Hermann Oesterley

Shakespeare's jest Book

A hundred mery Talys, from the only perfect Copy known

Hermann Oesterley

Shakespeare's jest Book
A hundred mery Talys, from the only perfect Copy known

ISBN/EAN: 9783337055783

Printed in Europe, USA, Canada, Australia, Japan

Cover: Foto ©ninafisch / pixelio.de

More available books at **www.hansebooks.com**

Shakespeare's Jest Book.

A HUNDRED MERY TALYS,

FROM THE ONLY PERFECT

COPY KNOWN.

EDITED,

WITH INTRODUCTION AND NOTES,

BY

DR. HERMAN OESTERLEY.

LONDON:
JOHN RUSSELL SMITH,
SOHO SQUARE.
1866.

INTRODUCTION.

THE editor of the following pages, while engaged in the compoſition of a new catalogue of the proſe works of fiction preſerved in the Royal Library of the University in Göttingen, met with a perfect copy of the "C. Merry Tales," printed by John Raſtell in 1526. He poſtponed, however, all reſearches regarding it until the time when the advancement of his work ſhould require. In the mean time this copy came under the notice of Dr. Carl Goedeke, the eminent judge of early literature, who at once recognized it as the book alluded to by Shakeſpeare in "Much Ado About Nothing." This cauſed my learned colleague, Prof. F. W. Unger, to give a bibliographical account of the diſcovery in the "Serapeum" (No. 9, May 15th, 1864, p. 142). About this time, Mr. Hazlitt's reprint

INTRODUCTION.

from the fragmentary but until this time only known copy reached us,[1] and notice was given of it in the "Göttinger gelehrte Anzeigen" (23 St. June 8th, 1864, p. 917) by Prof. Unger, thus again drawing the attention of literary men to the perfect copy preserved in our library.

The original of Mr. Hazlitt's edition was discovered by the Rev. J. J. Conybeare in 1815,[2] and reprinted the same year in S. W. Singer's "Jeſt Book."[3] It was printed without date,

[1] "Shakeſpeare Jeſt Books; reprints of the early and very rare Jeſt Books ſuppoſed to have been uſed by Shakeſpeare. I. A Hundred Mery Talys. II. Mery Tales and Quicke Anſweres. Edited, with Introduction and Notes, by W. Carew Hazlitt. London, Willis and Sotheran, 1864, 8º."

[2] Collier, "Shakeſpeare," Lond. 1842, vol. ii. p. 208, note 8, gives erroneouſly the year 1835 as the date of the diſcovery and reprint.

[3] "Shakeſpeare Jeſt Book. Part I. Tales and quicke Anſweres very mery and pleaſant to rede, with a Preface and a Gloſſary. Part II. A C mery Talys, with a Preface and Gloſſary. Part III. Supplement to the Tales and quicke Anſweres, being Mery Tales, wittie Queſtions and quicke Anſweres, very pleaſant to be readde." Chiſwick, 1814-16, 8vo. Three parts in 1 vol., 250 copies printed, with an "Addreſs to the Reader," by the editor, S. W. Singer, Eſq. Of this edition hardly a ſingle copy has ever come to Germany. See "Biographical Memoir of Edmond Malone" [by James Boſwell], Lond. 1814, privately

INTRODUCTION.   v

but with the mark of John Raſtell[4] on the reverſe of the laſt leaf, twenty-four leaves in folio, black letter.[5] Many leaves of this copy, from having been uſed as paſteboard to another book, were mutilated, and though ſeveral copies had been employed in faſhioning the paſteboard, and ſo a comparatively large fragment was ſaved, yet many deficiencies remained. Beſides a quantity of ſmaller gaps throughout the whole book, in twenty-ſix[6] of the tales ſeveral lines are wanting, and ſix[7] are too much damaged to decypher.

The original of the preſent edition is perfect. It was printed by John Raſtell in 1526, black letter, twenty-eight leaves in folio, though only

---

printed; "Retroſpective Review," N. S. No. 8, Aug. 1854, vol. ii. p. 313; "London Magazine," edited by Taylor and Heſſey, 1823-24.

[4] See, about this early Engliſh printer, James Ames, "Typographical Antiquities," augmented by W. Herbert, Lond. 1785-90, 4to. vol. i. p. 326.

[5] Lowndes, "The Bibliographer's Manual," part v. p. 1200, mentions the 18mo. ſize. For further particulars, ſee Mr. Hazlitt's edition, Introduction, p. iii. ſeq.

[6] Viz. Nos. 3, 4, 22, 24, 42, 46, 47, 49, 52, 53, 55, 59, 60, 63, 64, 67, 69, 74, 77, 81, 83, 87, 91, 94, 96, 100.

[7] Viz. Nos. 26, 35, 72, 78, 84, 95, correſponding to Nos. 28, 36, 74, 80, 86, 99 of this edition.

twenty-fix numbered, including title and table. It contains E iii by fignatures, the firft fheet in fours, the remainder in fixes. The front of the firft leaf is without fignature and bears in xylographic frame-work the title, " A .C. mery talys;" on the back of the leaf begins " the kalender" or the table of the tales, which is continued on the fecond leaf A ii. Then follow folios 1 to 26,[1] containing the text of the tales. The ftories are without headings or numbers, generally with a moral attached and a break in type between each. The firft letter of each ftory is printed feparately, moft of them in a fquare for illumination. The text finifhes upon the firft page of the laft leaf with the word " Finis;" on the reverfe follows the Colophon and the mark of *John Raftell* in large framework, and under it : *Cum preuilegio Regali.*

According to an entry in the Library's Manual of the year 1768[2] this copy has been purchafed at an auction of books in Lüneburg, December,

[1] Fol. 2 and 26 bear erroneoufly the numbers 26 and refp. 21.

[2] "Manuale," 1768. Angekommen d. 13 Jan. p. 6. Aus der Auction eines Vorraths von Büchern, welche am 7 Dec. 1767 u. f. zu Lüneburg in Peterfens Haufe an den Meiftbietenden follen verkauft werden, p. 9, 145, No. 2. " A C mery talys." Lond. 1526, (Acc. f. 5368.)

INTRODUCTION.   vii

1767; but I have been unsuccessful in tracing its history further back.

The differences between this impression and the one edited by Singer and reprinted by Mr. Hazlitt are very considerable. Our edition has four tales which are not contained in the undated copy, viz. Nos. 2, 7, 91 and 98; for which at the end of the latter three new stories are added, Nos. 97, 99 and 100. No. 98 is wanting in the table as well as in the text of Mr. Hazlitt's edition, and as he does not give any reason of this striking deficiency, nor even mention it, I am unable to decide whether it arises from a negligence of the original compiler, from a lacuna in the only preserved copy, or from an error of the later editors; the less, as Mr. Singer's reprint is said to be nearly an accurate facsimile of the original, and Mr. Hazlitt professes to have rigidly adhered even to the old orthography.

Again, in Mr. Hazlitt's edition the morals of Nos. 54, 79 and 96 are wanting, corresponding to Nos. 35, 81 and 100 of the present edition; and further is No. 43 of our original No. 33 of the undated copy.

For smaller variations I may first refer to the kalender or table. In the beginning the headings are entirely different, but afterwards, with the exception perhaps of Nos. 44 and 66 (Nos. 42

and 64 in Haz.), only very trifling alterations of single words occur.

The variations of the two editions in single phrases and expressions of the text are numerous, and they are, after careful collation, noted under the text, excepting those, however, which have arisen from the interpolations of the later editors.

Finally, the difference of orthography and punctuation might be mentioned, but for the capriciousness of the orthography in both editions, and for the thorough modernizing of the punctuation in Mr. Hazlitt's edition, the only one at my command.

The question, which of the two copies recovered up to the present moment is the original and older edition (and there is very little hope of ever discovering a third copy), will be very difficult to prove to an absolute certainty. By the want of any authentic indication, the inquiry is thrown back on a mere circumstantial proof; but I think the reasons to be given hereafter will be strong enough to produce a firm conviction of the priority of our original.

The first argument in favour of the edition of 1526 is founded on the selection and disposition of the tales. When a reprint of a collection of a hundred tales like the one in question is being prepared, and the removing of four stories seems desirable, it is unlikely enough, that the three or four last pieces should be cast off; but it is much more unlikely that the number required to complete a hundred should be inserted in entirely chance places. This, however, would have been the case in the Nos. 2, 7, 91 and 98 of our edition, if it had been a revision of the undated copy. On the other hand, it is quite natural simply to throw out the tales considered as unserviceable (which, as before mentioned, would hardly be placed together, but be scattered throughout the work) and to subjoin the additions at the end. This has been the case, if the undated edition is the result of a revision: Nos. 2, 7, 91 and 98 of the original edition have been suppressed, and in their stead Nos. 97 to 100 of the later impression are added. I must say, that this mode of revision, in a work where the disposition of the matter is entirely arbitrary, seems to me more natural than even putting the new stories in the place of the old ones. The substance of the tales in discussion can be of no moment for the question, for indeed, the one is about as insipid as the other, and moreover, the taste of our ancestors in regard to jests and popular tales was so very different from ours, that it is next to impossible at present to decide which of them might be confidered more palatable to the public at that time.

The tranfpofition of a fingle tale to another place[1] can, of courfe, be no conclufive argument either for one view or for the other, whereas the want of the morals in the undated copy is of confequence, if it really be found in the original and not be produced by a defect, which is not quite evident in Mr. Hazlitt's reprint. As our copy contains twenty-eight leaves and the undated one only twenty-four, therefore the arrangement of the type in each muft have been quite different; the abfence of thefe morals might have arifen from a defire of faving fpace, and thus furnifh a new evidence for the priority of the dated edition.

The variations in the table favour my opinion in an equal manner. Wherever any effential differences occur in the headings, they are equal to as many emendations in the undated copy,[2] and thefe improvements evidently bear witnefs to the later appearance of the revifed edition; the more, as there is no trace of a third edition earlier than both, of which the undated copy might poffibly be a revifed impreffion, ours being only a later and unrevifed reprint.

[1] No. 43 to No. 33 of the undated edition.
[2] See the headings of Nos. 1 to 6, 44 and 66.

This might, indeed, have been the cafe for the alterations of the text; but under the circumſtances it is too improbable to be advanced as an objection, and I may fairly put it out of the queſtion. Among the very large quantity of variations in the text, there are, of courſe, many entirely irrelevant in the deciſion of the queſtion, as they cannot be conſidered as improvements. The greater part, nevertheleſs, proves that the undated edition is the product of a reviſion. In the firſt place the miſprints are important. The typographical errors of our edition, about fifty or ſixty, have all been corrected in Mr. Hazlitt's original, in which, however, there are about twenty new miſprints. The moſt remarkable of theſe is p. 35, l. 13 of Mr. Hazlitt's reprint, where evidently from the repetition of the words "tyed faſt by the leggys" in three conſecutive lines (at the top of fol. vi verſo of our original) more than a line of our text has been omitted, the paſſage ending with the firſt repetition of thoſe words being left out. As it would be impoſſible to enumerate all the paſſages which go to prove my propoſition, I mention only ſome of the moſt ſtriking inſtances. Fol. 1 verſo, l. 39, the words "his neck," accidentally omitted in ours, are ſupplied in Mr. Hazlitt's edition; fol. 2 verſo, l. 10, "for that that"—Hazl. "becauſe;" fol. 10,

l. 38, " by vyolence "—Hazl. " of the houſe;" fol. 11 verſo, l. 16, " thy "—Hazl. " your;" fol. 14, l. 27, " vp through "—Hazl. " throughe it," &c; but eſpecially fol. 21, l. 3 and 4, a very corrupt paſſage of our text has been corrected in Mr. Hazlitt's edition, p. 102, l. 8; fol. 23, l. 2, the words " ſayde in ſporte " are omitted, but have been inſerted in the undated copy.

On the other hand, I feel obliged to mention that a few of the variations in the undated copy cannot well be conſidered as corrections from our text, but rather ſeem to indicate the reverſe;[1] this, however, is eaſily enough accounted for by the fact that alterations are not always improvements: indeed, in one inſtance[2] the very corruption of the text proves its being a reviſed edition.

The orthography in both editions is too varied and unſettled to be of any moment for our queſtion, although the frequent uſe of written numbers in the undated copy inſtead of the ſimple cypher, and perhaps the employing of the word " pence " for our abbreviation d. ſeem to ſtrengthen my argument. On the whole, all

---

[1] F. e. fol. 12, l. 34; fol. 12 verſo, l. 27; fol. 16 verſo, l. 23; fol. 20, l. 21, &c.

[2] Fol. 20 verſo, l. 9; ſee the notes.

the orthography proves is that only a few years elapfed between the appearance of the two editions.

Thefe are the arguments I have to prefent; although each taken fingly may not be confidered conclufive, the whole will form as unexceptionable a proof of the priority of our edition as can be expected, and this proof is the more cogent, as there is nothing worth mentioning to be offered in favour of the other edition.

The notes added to the prefent edition do not in any way pretend to contain all that might be collated in regard to the fources and imitations of the "C Mery Talys." It has certainly been my endeavour to make this collection of parallels as entire as poffible, but, of courfe, it was only the material at my command which I could call into requifition; and although this material was uncommonly copious, I have no doubt in a complete collection, efpecially of Englifh Jeft Books, much more might have been gathered. However, many of the Merry Tales bear too unmiftakeably the ftamp of originality to leave any hope of tracing their origin farther, and a large number we may fafely fuppofe have never been transferred to the collections of a later period. This forms the effential diftinction between the prefent and moft of the other Englifh Jeft Books, ours being the only one (within my knowledge, at leaſt) containing tales upon the origin or difſemination of which authentic information cannot be obtained.

It only remains for me to expreſs my ſincereſt thanks to my learned friend, Dr. Carl Goedeke, for the highly valuable aſſiſtance he has furniſhed me in the accompliſhment of my work.

CONTENTS.

	Page
I. Of the mylner that fayd he harde neuer but of ii commaundemens and .ii. dowtys	1
II. Of the cytefen that callyd the preſt ſyr Johñ & he callyd him maſter raf	2
III. Of the wyfe that mayd hyr huſbande to go ſyt in the herber in the nyght while her prentys lay with her in her bed	3
IV. Of hym that playd the deuyll and came thorow the waren & mayd theym that ſtale the connys to ronne away	7
V. Of the ſyk man that bequethyd hys thyrd ſon a lytyll ground with the galows	11
VI. Of the gentylman that loſt his ryng in the gentylwomans bed, & a nother gentylman found it after in the ſame bed	13
VII Of the huſband man that aſked for maſter pyſpot the phyſyſyon	14
VIII. Of the ſcoler that bare his ſhoys to cloutyng	17
IX. Of hym that ſayd that a womans tong was lightiſt met of degeſtion	18
X. Of the woman that folowyd her fourth huſbandys herce & wept	19

CONTENTS.

		Page
XI.	Of the woman that fayd her wooer came too late	20
XII	Of the mylner with the golden thombe	22
XIII.	Of the horfman of yrelond that prayd Oconer to hang vp the frere	22
XIV.	Of the preft that fayd nother corpus meus nor corpum meum	25
XV.	Of the .ii. frerys wherof the one louyd not the ele hed nor the other the tayle	26
XVI.	Of the welchman that fhroue hym for brekyng his faft on the fryday	27
XVII.	Of the merchaunt of london that put nobles in his mouth in his deth bed	30
XVIII.	Of the mylner that ftale the nuttys & of the tayler that ftale a fhepe	31
XIX.	Of the .iiii. elementys where they fhulde fone be found	37
XX.	Of the woman that powryd the potage in the Juggys male	39
XXI.	Of the weddyd men that cam to heuyn to clayme theyr herytage	41
XXII.	Of the merchaunte that chargyd hys fonne to fynde one to fynge for hys fowle	42
XXIII.	Of the mayd wafhyng clothys and anfwered the frere	44
XXIV.	Of the .iii. wyfe men of gotam	45
XXV.	Of the gray frere that anfweryd his penytent	47
XXVI.	Of the gentylman that bare the fege borde on his nek	47
XXVII.	Of the marchauntys wyfe that feyd fhe wolde take a nap at fermon	51
XXVIII.	Of the woman that feyd & fhe lyffyd a nother yere fhe wolde haue a kokoldis hat of her owne	52

CONTENTS.

XXIX.	Of the gentylman that wyſhyd his toth in the gentylwomans tayle	53
XXX.	Of the welchman that confeſſyd hym how he had ſlayn a frere	54
XXXI.	Of the welchman that cowde not get but a lytyll male	55
XXXII.	Of the gentyll woman that ſayd to a gentylman ye haue a berde a boue & none benethe	57
XXXIII.	Of the frere that ſayd our lord fed .v. M. peple with .ij. fyſhys	58
XXXIV.	Of the frankelyne that wold haue had the frere gon	59
XXXV.	Of the good man that ſayd to his wyfe he had yll fare	60
XXXVI.	Of the frere that bad hys chylde make a laten	61
XXXVII.	Of the gentylman that aſkyd the frere for his beuer	62
XXXVIII.	Of the .iii. men that chaſe the woman . .	63
XXXIX.	Of the gentylman that taught his cooke the medeſyne for the tothake	65
XL.	Of the gentylman that promyſyd the ſcoler of Oxford a ſarcenet typet	67
XLI.	Of maſter ſkelton that brought the byſhop of Norwich .ii. feſantys	70
XLII.	Of the yeman of gard that ſayd he wold bete the carter	73
XLIII.	Of the pryſt that ſayd our lady was not ſo curyous a woman	75
XLIV.	Of the fole that wold go to the deuyll . .	76
XLV.	Of the plowmannys ſonne that ſayd he ſaw one make a Goſe to kreke ſweetly . . .	77

b

CONTENTS.

		Page
XLVI.	Of the maydys anfwere that was with chylde	78
XLVII.	Of the feruant that rymyd with his mafter	79
XLVIII.	Of the welchman that delyueryd the letter to the ape	81
XLIX.	Of hym that fold ryght nought	83
L.	Of the frere that told the iii. chylders fortunys	86
LI.	Of the boy that bare the frere hys mafters money	88
LII.	Of Phylyp fpencer the bochers man	89
LIII.	Of the courtear and the carter	91
LIV.	Of the yonge man that prayd his felow to tech hym his pater nofter	91
LV.	Of the frere that prechyd in ryme expownyng the aue maria	93
LVI.	Of the curat that prechyd the artycles of the Crede	96
LVII.	Of the frere that prechyd the .x. comaundementys	100
LVIII.	Of the wyfe that bad her hufband ete the candell furft	103
LIX.	Of the man of lawys fonnys anfwer	104
LX.	Of the frere in the pulpit that bad the woman leue her babelyng	104
LXI.	Of the welchman that caft the fkot in to the fee	106
LXII.	Of the man that had the dome wyfe	107
LXIII.	Of the proctor of arches that had the lytell wyfe	109
LXIV.	Of the .ii. nonnys that were fhryuyn of one preft	110
LXV.	Of the efquyer that fholde haue bene made knyght	112

CONTENTS.

		Page
LXVI.	Of the man that wold haue the pot ſtand there as he wold	114
LXVII.	Of the penytent that ſayd the ſhepe of god haue mercy vpon me.	116
LXVIII.	¶ Of the huſband that ſayd he was Johñ daw	117
LXIX.	¶ Of the ſkoler of oxford that prouyd by ſoupheſtry .ii. chekyns .iii.	118
LXX.	¶ Of the frere that ſtale the podyng . .	120
LXXI.	Of the frankelyns ſon that cam to take orders	122
LXXII.	Of the huſbandman that lodgyd the frere in hys owne bed	124
LXXIII.	Of the preſt that wold ſay .ii. goſpels for a grote	125
LXXIV.	Of the courtear that dyd caſt the frere ouer the bote.	126
LXXV.	Of the frere that prechyd what mennys ſowlys were.	127
LXXVI.	Of the huſband that cryed ble vnder the bed	128
LXXVII.	Of the ſhomaker that aſkyd the colyer what tydyngys in hell	130
LXXVIII.	Of ſeynt Peter that cryed cauſe bobe . .	131
LXXIX.	Of hym that aduenturyd body & ſowle for hys prynce	132
LXXX.	Of the parſon that ſtall the mylners elys .	133
LXXXI.	Of the welchman that ſaw one .xl. ſhyl. better than god	134
LXXXII.	Of the frere that ſayd dyrige for the hoggys ſowle.	134
LXXXIII.	Of the parſon that ſayd maſſe of requiem for Cryſtys ſowle	136

		Page
LXXXIV.	Of the herdman that fayd ryde apace ye fhall haue rayn	138
LXXXV.	Of hym that fayd I fhall haue nere a peny	139
LXXXVI.	Of the hufband that fayd his wyfe and he agreed well	140
LXXXVII.	Of the preeft that fayd comede epifcope .	141
LXXXVIII	Of the woman that ftale the pot . . .	142
LXXXIX.	Of mafter whyttyntons dreme	143
XC.	Of the preft that kyllyd hys horfe callyd modicum	144
XCI.	Of the maltman of Colbroke . . .	145
XCII.	Of the welchman that ftale the englyfhmans cok	150
XCIII.	Of hym that brought a botell to a preft .	150
XCIV.	Of the endytement of Jhefu of Nazareth .	151
XCV.	Of hym that prechyd agaynft theym that rode on the fonday	152
XCVI.	Of the one brother that founde a purs .	153
XCVII.	Of the anfwere of the mafters to the mayd	155
XCVIII.	Of a certayn aldermans dedys of london .	155
XCIX.	Of the northern man that was all hart .	158
C.	Of the burnyng of old Johñ	158

A HUNDRED MERY TALYS.

1. *Of the mylner that fayd he harde neuer but of ii commaũdemens and .ii. dowtys.*

 CERTAYN Curat in the contrey there was that preched in the pulpit of the ten commandementys. Seyng that there were ten cõmaũdemētes that euery man ought to kepe/ & he that brake any of thẽ/ cõmytted greuous fyn/[1] how be it he fayd that fomtyme it was dedly fyn & fomtyme venyall/ But when it was dedly fyn & when venyall/ there were many douts therin. And a mylner a yong mã a mad felow that cam feldom to church/[2] & had ben at very fewe fermons or none in all his lyfe anfwerd hym thã fhortly this wyfe. I meruel mafter parfon that ye fay ther be fo many cõmaũdemētis & fo many doutys. For I neuer hard tell but of ii.

[1] *greuous fyn*] Hazl. fyn. [2] *church*] Orig. reads chnrch.

cõmandemẽts that is to ſay cõmande me to you and cõmaũde me fro you. Nor I neuer herd tell of mo[1] doutis but twayn that ys to ſay dout[2] the candell and dout the fyre. At which anſwere all the people fell a laughynge.

¶ By this tale a man may well pceyue that they that be brought vp without lernyng[3] or good maner ſhall neuer be but rude and beſtely all though they haue good naturall wyttys.

11. *Of the cyteſen that callyd the preſt ſyr Johñ & he called hĩ maſter raf.*
Wanting in Hazlitt's edition.

N a tyme there was a Joly Citeſyn walkyng in the cõtrey for ſport which met with a folyſh preſt/ & in diryſyõ in cõmunycaciõ cald hym ſyr Johñ. this preſt vnderſtonding his mockyng calde him maſter rafe/ why quod the cyteſyn doſte thou call me maſter rafe/ mary quod the preſt why callyſt me ſyr Johñ. Then quod the cyteſen I call the ſyr Johñ becawſe euery folyſh preſte moſt comonly is calde ſir John/ Mary quod the preſt & I call the maſter rafe becauſe eueryproud

---

[1] *mo*] Hazl. more.   [2] *dout*] i. e. fear.
[3] *vp without lernyng*] Orig. reads vpwith out leryng.

Cocold moſt comenly is callyd maſter Rafe. At the which anſwer all that were by laught a pace becauſe dyuers there ſuppoſyd the ſame cyteſen to be a cokcold in dede.

¶ By thys tale ye may ſe that he that delyteth[4] to deryde & laughe other to ſkorne is ſomtyme hym ſelfe more derydyd.

III. *Of the wyfe that mayd hyr huſbande to go ſyt in the herber in the nyght whyle her prentys lay with her in her bed.*

The ſources as well as the imitations of this ſtory are very numerous. It ſeems to be modelled after Boccaccio, "Il Decamerone," giorn. vii. nov. 7, or perhaps after the "Cent Nouvelles Nouvelles," nouv. 88. But its real origin is a French fabliau, either "La bourgeoiſe d'Orléans," in Legrand d'Auſſy, "Fabliaux ou Contes du XII. et du XIII. ſiècle," Paris, 1779, tom. iii. p. 411 (alſo in Barbazan-Méon, "Fabliaux et Contes," Paris, 1808, p. 161); or "Raymond Vidal," in Raynouard, "Choix des Poéſies originales des Troubadours," Paris, 1816-1819, tom. iii. p. 398. Likewiſe it is contained in "Poggii facetiæ," s. l. & a. fol: "de muliere quæ virum defraudavit," fol. v. verſo; in Mone's "Anzeiger für Kunde des deutſchen Mittelalters," iv. 453; "Der Herr und der Schreiber;" in Von der Hagen, "Geſammtabenteuer," No. 27; "Frauenbeſtaendigkeit," Bd. ii. Stuttgart & Tübingen, 1850; and in "Grimm," Deutſche Sagen, Bd. ii. Berlin, 1818, p. 186; "Kaiſer Heinrich verſucht die Kaiſerin."

[4] *delyteth*] Orig. reads delyteh.

A HUNDRED

The following are more or less exact imitations of these different sources: Henr. Bebelii "Facetiæ, additamenta Hermotimi," in Nicod. Frischlini "Facet. Selectiores," Amstelod. 1660, p. 313; Joh. Gastius, "Convivalium sermonum," Basil, 1549, tom. i. p. 198; Ser Giovanni Fiorentino, "Il Pecorone," giorn. iii. nov. 2; Celio Malespini, "Ducento novelle," nov. 61; Ludov. Domenichi, "Facetie," p. 204; Matteo Bandello, "Novelle," tom. ii. nov. 25; "Conti da ridere," tom. i. p. 139 "d'un uomo che fu cornuto, battuto e contento;" Timoneda, "Alivio de Caminantes," p. i. No. 69, reprinted in "Bibl. de Aut. Español." vol. iii. p. 175; "Romanzero general," Madrid, 1614, p. ix. fol. 344; H. Estienne (Henr. Stephanus) "Apologie pour Hérodote, augm. de remarques par Le Duchat," La Haye, 1735, tom. i. chap. 15, p. 279; Dancourt, "Oeuvres," Paris, 1729; tom. ii. No. 1, "Le tuteur;" "Roger Bontems en belle humeur," Cologne, 1731, tom. i. p. 55: "D'un homme qui fut cocu, battu et content;" "Contes à rire, ou Récréations Françaises," ed. 1787, tom. ii. p. 130; Lafontaine, Contes: "Le Cocu battu et content," liv. i. c. 3; B. Waldis, "Esopus," iv. 81; Joh. Pet. de Memel, "Lustige Gesellschaft" (imperfect copy of the Library in Göttingen), No. 2, f. 26; Philander, "Der Kurzweilige Zeitverkürzer," s. l. 1702, No. 481, p. 323; A. F. E. Langbein, Schwänke: "Der Kammerdiener," ed. 1765, Bd. i. p. 29; "A Sackful of Newes," London, 1673, reprinted in Mr. Hazlitt's "Shakespeare Jest-Books," 2nd series, Lond. 1864, p. 169.

A WYFE ther was which had apointed her prētys to com to her bed in the night which seruāt had long woyd her to haue his plesure which acordīge to the apoītmēt

cā to her bed ſyde ī the night her huſbād liyng by her & when ſhe ꝑceyuyd hym ther ſhe caught hī by the hād & hyld hym faſt & incōtinēt wakened her huſbŏd & ſayd/ Sir it is ſo ye haue a fals & an vntrue ſeruāt to you which is william your prentys & has lōge woyd me to haue his pleſur/ & becawſe I coud nat auoyde his importunate requeſt I haue appoītyd hym this night to met me in the gardē ī the herber & yf ye wyll aray your ſelf in myn aray & go theder ye ſhall ſe the ꝓfe therof & then ye may rebuke hym as ye thīke beſt by your dyſcrecyon/ this huſbād thus aduertiſed by his wyfe/ put vpō hym his wyues raymēt[1] & went to the herber and when he was gone thyder the prentys cā in to bed to his maſtres wher for a ſeaſō they wer both contētt and pleaſyd ech other by the ſpace of an hour or .ij. but when ſhe thought tyme cōuenyēt ſhe ſayd to the prentyſe Now go thy way in to the herber & mete hym & take a good waſter[2] in thy hād & ſay thou dydys it but to ꝓue whether I woldbe a good womā or no & reward hym as thou thynkyſt beſt. This prentys doïg after his maſtres cōcell wēt to[3] the herber wher he founde his maſter ī his maſtres appel & ſayd A thou

---

[1] *rayment*] Orig. reads raymtē.
[2] *waſter*] i.e. cudgel.
[3] *went to*] Hazl. went in to.

harlot art thou comẽ hether/ now I ſe well yf I wold be fals to my maſter thou woldeſt be a ſtrõg hore but I had leuer thou wer hãgyd thã I wold do him ſo traterous a dede therfore I ſhall gyve the ſome puniſhment as thou lyke an hore haſt deſeruyd/ & therwith lapt hĩ well about the ſholds & bak and gaue hym a doſẽ or .ii. good ſtrypys the maſter felyng hym ſelfe sõwhat to ſmart ſayd peſe wylliã myne own true good ſeruãt for godys ſake hold thy hãdys for I ã thi maſter & not thi maſtres/ na hore quod he thou lyeſt thou art but an harlot & I dyd but to pue the/ & ſmote hĩ agayn. Alas man quod the maſter I beſeche the nomore for I am not ſhe for I am thy maſter fele for I haue a berd/ and therwith he ſparyd his hãd & felt hys berd. Alas maſter[1] quod the prentys I crye you mercy & then the mayſter went vnto hys wyfe & ſhe aſkyd hym how he had ſped & he ãſwerd I wis[2] wyfe I haue bene ſhrewdly betyn how be it I haue cauſe to be glad for I thanke god I haue as trew a wyfe & as trew a ſeruant as any man hath in englond.

¶ By this tale ye may ſe that it is not wyſdome for a man to be rulyd alway after hys wyues councell.

[1] *Alas maſter*] Hazl. good mayſter.
[2] *I wis*] i. e. I know.

IV. *Of hym that playd the deuyll and came thorow the waren & mayd theym that ſtale the connys to ronne away.*

IT fortunyd that in a market towne in the counte of Suffolk there was a ſtage play ĩ the which playe on callyd Johñ adroyns wich dwelyd ĩ a nother vyllage ij. myle frõ thẽs playd the deuyll. And whẽ the play was done this Johñ adroyns ĩ the euenyng departyd fro the ſayd market towne to go home to his owne houſe & be cauſe³ he had there no chãge of clothĩge he went forth ĩ his deuylls apell whiche ĩ the way comyng homward cã thorow a waren of conys belõgyng to a gẽtylmã of the vyllage wher he hym ſelfe dwelt. at which tyme it fortunyd a preſt a vycar of a church therby with ij. or iij. other vnthryfty felowes had brought with thẽ a hors a hey & a feret to thẽtẽt ther to get conis & whẽ the feret was in the yerth & the hey⁴ ſet ouer the path way wherĩ⁵ thys Johñ adroyns ſhold com. this preſt & this⁶ other felowes ſaw hym com ĩ the deuyls raymẽt cõſyderĩg that they were ĩ the deuyls ſeruyſe & ſtelĩg of cones & ſuppoſynge it had ben the deuyll in dede for

---

³ *& be cauſe*] Hazl. becauſe.   ⁴ *a hey*] i. e. a net.
⁵ *wherin*] Hazl. where.   ⁶ *& this*] Hazl. and his.

fere ran away. this John adroyns ĩ the deuyls raymẽt & be caufe it was fõwhat dark faw not the hey but wẽt forth ĩ haft & ftõblid therat & fell down & wyth¹ the fall he had almoft broke his nek.²

But whẽ he was a lytyll reuyuyd he lokyd vp & fpyed it was a hay to chach connys & lokyd further/ & faw that they ran away for fere of hym/ & faw a horfe tyed to a bufh laden with connys whych they had taken/ & he toke the horfe & the haye & lepe³ vpõ the horfe & rode to the gentylmannys place that was lorde of the waren/ to the entente to haue thanke for takynge fuche a pray. And when he cam/ knokyd at the gatys. To whome anone one of gentylmannys feruauntys afkyd who was there/ and fodeynly openyd the gate/ and affone as he perceyuyd hym in the deuyls raymente was fodenly abafhyd/ and fparryd the dore agayn/ & went in to his mayf-ter/ and fayd & fware to hys mayfter that the deuyll was at the gate/ and wolde come in. The gentylman heryng hym fay fo callyd another of hys feruaũntys & bad hym go to the gate to knowe who was there. This feconde feruaũt

---

& *wyth* Hazl. that with.
² The words *his nek* in orig. accidentally are omitted.
³ *lepe*] Hazl. lept.

cam to the gate durſt not open it/ but aſkyd with
lowd voyce who was there. thys Johñ Adroyns[4]
in the deuyls apperell anſwerd with a hye voyce
and ſayd/ Tell thy maſter I muſt nedys ſpeke
with hym or[5] I go. This fecõd feruaũt heryng
that anſwer ſuppoſynge alſo it had bene the deuyll/
went in agayn to his maſter and ſayd thus/
mayſter yt is the deuyll in dede that ys at the
gate/ and ſayth he muſt nedys ſpeke with you or
he go hens. The gentylmã then began a lyttvll
to baſhe and callyd the ſteward of hys howſe/
whyche was the wyſyſt feruaunt that he had and
bad hym to go to the gate and to brynge hym
ſure worde who was there. This ſteward be
cauſe he thaught he wold ſe ſurely who was there
came to the gate and lokyd thorow the chinys of
the gate in dyuers placys/ and ſaw well that yt
was the deuyll and ſat vpon an horſe and hangynge aboute the ſaddell on euery ſyde ſawe the
cony heddys hengynge down/ than he came to
his mayſter aferde in greate haſte and ſayd/ By
goddys body yt is the deuyll in dede that is at the
gate ſyttyng vpon an horſe laden all wyth
ſowllys/ and by lykelyhede/[6] he is com for your

[4] *Adroyns*] Orig. reads Androyns.
[5] *or*] i. e. ere, before.
[6] *by lykelyhede*] Hazl. be lykelyhode.

foule[1] purpofely/ and lakkyth but your foule/ &
yf he had your fowle I wene[2] he fhold be gone.
This gentylman thã meruelously abafhyd callyd
vp[3] his chapleyn/ and made the holy candell to be
lyght/ and gat holy water and wente to the gate
wyth as many of hys feruauntys as durfte go with
hym/ where the chaplayn with holy wordys of
coniuracyon fayde/ In the name of the fader/
fonne and holy gooft/ I coniure the and charg
the in the holy name of god to tell me why and
wherfore thowe commyfte hyther.

This Johñ Androynys in the deuyllys apparell
heryng theym begynne to cõiure after fuche maner
fayd/ Nay nay be not a ferd of me for I am a good
dyuell I am Johñ Adroyns your neghboour dwellyng in thys towne[4] and he that played the dyuell/
to day in the play/ I haue braught my mayfter a
dofen or ii.[5] of hys owne connyes that were ftolyn
in hys waren and theyr horfe & theyr hay/ and
made theym for fere to ronne away/ and when
they[6] herde hym thus fpeke by hys voyce they
knew hym well ynoughe[7] and openyd the gate

---

[1] *foule*] in orig. fonle.   [2] *I wene*] I fuppofe.
[3] *callyd vp*] Hazl. called.
[4] *dwellyng in thys towne*] Hazl. in this towne.
[5] *ii.*] Hazl. two.
[6] *and when they*] Hazl. whanne they.
[7] *they knew hym well ynoughe*] Hazl. knewe him well.

and let hym come in/ And ſo all the forſayd fere and dred⁸ was tornyd to myrth and dyſporte.

¶ By this tale ye may ſe that mẽ fear many tymes more than they nede which hath cauſyd mẽ to beleue that ſpyryttys & deuyls haue bene ſene in dyuers placys when it hath bene nothynge ſo.

v. *Of the ſyk man that bequethyd hys thyrd ſon a lytyll ground with the galows.*

THER was a riche man which lay ſore ſeke in his bed lyke to dy⁹ wherfore his eldyſt ſon cam to hym & beſechyd hym to gyue hym his blyſſyng to whom the fader ſayd ſon thou ſhalt haue goddys bleſſyng & myne and for that that¹⁰ thou haſt ben euer good of cõdycyons I gyue & bequeth the all my land/ to whom he anſwered & ſayd nay fad I truſt you ſhal lyue & occupy them your ſelfe full well by goddys grace. Sone after came his ij. ſone¹¹ to hym lyke wyſe & deſyred his bleſſyng/ to whom the fad ſayd becauſe¹² thou haſt be¹³ euer kynde

---

⁸ *fere and dred*] Hazl. feare.
⁹ *lyke to dy*] Hazl. to (deth).
¹⁰ *for that that*] Hazl. becauſe.
¹¹ *his ij. ſone*] Hazl. another ſonne.
¹² *becauſe*] Hazl. my ſonne.   ¹³ *be*] Hazl. ben.

& gentyll[1] & I geue the goddys bleſſynge & myn and alſo[2] I bequeth the all my mouable goodys/ to whom he anſwerd and ſayd/ nay fader I truſt ye ſhall lyve & do well & ſpend and vſe your goodys your ſelfe by goddys grace. Anon after the iij. ſone cam to hym & deſyred his bleſſyng to whom the fader anſwerd & ſayd by cauſe thou haſt bene euyll & ſtoborne of condycyons & wolde neuer be ruled after my coūſell I haue nother land nor goodys onbequethyd but onely a lytell vacant ground wher a galows ſtandyth which now I geue and bequeth to the/ and goddys curſe withall/ to whom the ſonne anſwerd as hys bretherne dyd & ſayd nay fader I truſt ye ſhall lyue and be in good helth and haue yt and occupy it your ſelfe by goddys grace. But after that the fader dyed & this thyrd ſon cōtynuyd ſtyll hys vnthryfty condycyons wherefore yt was hys fortune afterwarde for hys deſeruyng to be hangyd on the ſame galows.

¶ By this tale men may wel perceyue that yong people that wyll not be rulyd by theyr frendys councell in youth in tymys come to a ſhamfull ende.

[1] *gentyll &*] Hazl. gentyll.
[2] *and alſo*] Hazl. and.

VI. *Of the gentylman that loſt his ryng in the gentylwomans bed, & a nother gentylman found it after in the ſame bed.*

This tale is taken from the " Cent Nouvelles Nouvelles," nouv. 62. It is imitated by Celio Maleſpini in " Ducento novelle," nov. 2, and by Decker and Webſter in " Northward Hoe," 160 f, aɛt. 1, ſc. i. See Webſter's Works, ed. by A. *Dyce*. London, 1830, vol. iii. p. 139.

TWO gẽtylmen of accoyntaũce wer appoyntyd to ly with a gẽtyll[3] womã in one nyght[4] the one not knowĩge of the other at dyuers tymis. This fyrſt at[5] his houre appoyntyd cã/ & in the bed ther he fortunid to leſe a ryng/ the .ij.[6] gentylmã when he was gone cam/ & fortunyd to fynd the ſame rynge/ & when he had ſped hys beſynes departyd/ & .ij. or .iii.[7] dayes after the furſt gẽtylman ſeyng hys ryng on the others fynger chalengyd yt[8] of hym & he[9] denyed yt hym & bad hĩ tell wher he had loſt it & he ſeyd ĩ ſuch a gentylwomans

---

[3] *gẽtyll*] Orig. reads gẽyll.
[4] *in one nyght*] Hazl. both in one nyght.
[5] *at*] Orig. reads ad.
[6] *the ij.*] Hazl. the ſeconde.
[7] *ij. or iii.*] Hazl. two or thre.
[8] *chalengyd yt*] Hazl. and chalenged it.
[9] *& he*] Orig. reads he &.

bed/ than quod the other & ther founde I yt/ & the one fayd he wolde haue yt/ the other fayd he fhulde not/ thã they agreyd to be iuggid by the next mã that they mote/¹ & it fortunid theym to mete with the hufbãd of the fayd gentyll womã & defyryd hym of his beft Jugemēt fhowyng hym all hole² mater/ then quod he by my iugemēt he that owd³ the fhetys fhould haue the ryng/ thē quod they & for your good iugemēt you fhall haue the ryng.

VII. *Of the hufband man that afkyd for mafter pyfpot the phyfyfyŏ.*

Wanting in Hazl. B. Waldis, "Efopus," iv. 23. In Jafander, "Der Teutfche Hiftorien Schreiber," Frankf. et Leipz. 1730, No. 128, p. 246, a fimilar ftory is related: a peafant afks for Dr. Lindwurm (Dragon) inftead of Dr. Drachen, &c. Jt. No. 27; Jt. Taylor, "Wit and Mirth," p. 101.

N a vyllage in fuffex there dwellyd a hufbandmã whofe wyfe fortunyd to fall fyk. Thys hufbandman came to the preeft of the church and defyryd hys councell

---

¹ *mote*] Hazl. dyd mete.
² *all hole*] Hazl. all the hole.
³ *owd*] Hazl. ought.

what thyng was beſt to help his wyfe/ whych anſweryd hym & ſayd y^t in bredſtrete in londõ there was a connyng Pheſycyon whoſe name is callyd maſter Jordayne/ Go to hym & ſhew hym that thy wyfe is ſyk and Jmpotent & not able to go & ſhew hym her water and beſeech hym to be good maſter to the/ and praye hym to do hys cure vppon her: and I warrant he wyll tech the ſome medſyne that ſhall help her. Thys huſbandman folowyng hys councell cã to london & aſkyd of dyuers men which was the way to good ale ſtrete[4] ſo y^t euery man y^t hard hym laught hym to ſcorne. At the laſt on y^t harde hym aſkyd him whether it were not bred ſtrete that he wold haue/ By god quod the huſbandmã ye ſay treuth: for I wyſt well it was other brede or drink: So whẽ they had taught hym the way to bred ſtrete & was ẽteryd into y^e ſtrete he aſkyd of dyuers men where one maſter Pyſpot dwellyd whych ſayd they knew no ſuch mã & laught at hym apace. At laſt one aſkyd him whether it were not maſter Jordayn ye phyſyciõ. ye y^e ſame quod ye huſbandmã for I wot well a iordayn & a pyſpot is all one. So whẽ they had ſhewyd hym hys houſe he wẽt thyder & cã to hym & dyd hys erãd thys & ſayd/ Syr if it

---

[4] *ſtrete*] Orig. reads ſtrere.

pleafe your mafhyp I vnderftand ye ar callyd a conyng confufyon : So it is my wyfe is fyk & omnypotent & may not go & here I haue brought you her water I befech you do your corage vppon her & I fhall gyue your mafhyp a good reward. The phefyciõ pfeynyng by the water y^t fhe was weke of nature bad hym get her mete y^t were reftoratyue & fpecyally if he coud let her haue a poũdgarnet & to let her not ouercome her ftomak w^t mych mete tyll fhe haue an apetyte. Thys hufbãdmã herd him fpeke of a poundgarnet & an apetite had wend he had fpoken of a pound of garlyk and of an ape & fhortly bought a pound of garlyk & after went to the ftylyard & bought an ape of one of the marchantys & brought both home to hys wyfe and tyed the ape w^t a cheyn at hys beddys fete/ & made hys wyfe to ete the pound of garlyk whether fhe wolde or no/ whereby fhe fell in fo great a lafk that it purgyd all the corrupciõ out of her body : whereby & by refõ y^t the ape that was tyde ther made fo many mokkys fkyppys & knakkys that made her oftymys to be mery & laugh that thankyd be god fhe was fhortly reftoryd to helth.

¶ By thys tale ye may fe that oft tymys medefyns taken at aduenturys do as mich good to the Pacyent as medefyns geuen by the folempne coũcell of conyng phyfycyons.

VIII. *Of the ſcoler that bare his ſhoys to cloutyng.*

A ſimilar affectation in "Neuvermehrte luſtige Pennal-Poſſen," s. l. & a. 8vo. ſign. E. 6.

IN the vnyuerſyte of Oxonford there was a ſkoler y^t delytyd mich to ſpeke eloquent engliſh & curious termis/ And cã to ye cobler wyth hys ſhoys whych were pikid before as they vſyd y^t feſon[1] to haue them cloutyd & ſayd thys wyſe/ Cobler I pray the ſet me .ii. tryangyls & .ii.[2] ſemy cercles vppon my ſubpedytals & I ſhall gyue the for thy labor/ This cobler[3] becauſe he vnderſtode hym not half well[4] ãſwerid ſhortly & ſayd/ Syr youre eloquence paſſith myne ītelligence/ but I promyſe you yf ye[5] meddyll wyth me/ the clowtyng of your ſhone ſhall coſte you .iij.[6] pence.

¶ By thys tale mē may lerne y^t it is foly to ſtudy to ſpeke eloquētly before them that be rude & vnlernyd.

[1] *as they vſyd that ſeſon*] Hazl. (as they uſed that tyme).
[2] *ij*] Hazl. two.
[3] *This cobler*] Hazl. The cobeler.
[4] *half well*] Hazl. halfe.
[5] *ye*] Hazl. he.
[6] *iij*] Hazl. thre.

IX. *Of him that ſayd that a womãs tong was lightiſt met of degeſtiõ.*

The ſource of this tale is Johannes de Bromyard, "Summa prædicantium," s. l. & a. fol. Litt. L. v. § 21, Exempl. i.: "Patet per hiſtoriam qua fertur infirmum reſpondiſſe medico dicenti: quod comederet de parte piſcium caude propinquiori: quia ſanior erat pars: quia plus mouebatur: ergo inquit infirmus: lingua uxoris mee ſaniſſima eſt, quia continue mouetur." Reprinted from a MS. in the Britiſh Muſeum in Th. Wright, "Latin Stories from MSS. of the 13th and 14th Centuries," London, 1842; (Percy Society, vol. viii.), No. 132: "De Linguis Mulierum."

Another verſion is found in Vincentii Bellovacenſis, "Speculum Morale," Duaci, 1624, fol. 86: "Narratvr de quodam, quod cum ipſe in mari haberet vxorem ſuam ſecum lingualam, grauem ad tolerandum: cum imminente tempeſtate clamatum eſſet a nautis, quod grauiora de naui proiicerentur, ille exhibuit vxorem dicens quod in tota naui non erat aliquid grauius lingua eius." It is imitated in H. Bebelii, "Facetiæ, opuſcula," s. l. & a. (circa 1512), 4°. ſign. Cc, verſo: "De quodam in tempeſtate maris deprehenſo (de alio)," and repeated in Joh. Gaſtius, "Convivalium Sermonum," tom. i. p. 281, Baſil, 1549.

A CERTAYN artificer in londõ there was which was ſore ſyk that coud not well dygeſt hys mete/ to whõ a phyſycõ cam to gyue hym councell & ſeyd y^t he muſt vſe to ete metis y^t be light of dygeſtyon as

ſmall byrdys/[1] as ſparous or ſwallous & eſpecyall[2] yᵗ byrd yᵗ ys callyd a wagtale whoſe fleſhe
ys meruelouſe lyght of dygeſtyõ becauſe that
byrd ys euer mouyng & ſtyryng. The ſik man
heryng the pheſicion ſeyd ſo anſweryd hym &
ſeyd/ Syr yf that be the cauſe yᵗ thoſe birdys be
lyght of dygeſtyon/ Than I know a mete mych
lyghter of dygeſtion thã other ſparow ſwallow or
wagtayle/ & that ys my wyuys tõg for it is neuer
in reſt but euer mouying & ſtyrryng.

¶ By thys tale ye may leſne a good generall
rule of pheſyk.

x. *Of the woman that folowyd her fourth huſbandys
berce & wept.*

A WOMAN ther was whych had had
.iiii. huſbãdes. It fortunyd alſo that
this fourth huſband died & was
brought to chirch vppon yᵉ bere/ whõ this womã
folowyd & made gret mone & wext very ſory. In
ſo mych that her neybours thought ſhe wold
ſowne & dy for ſorow/ wherfor one of her goſ-
ſyps cam to her & ſpake to her in her ere &

---

[1] *as ſmall byrdys*] Hazl. and ſmall byrdys.
[2] *eſpecyall*] Hazl. eſpecyally.

bad her for goddes fake to comfort[1] her felf &
refrayne that lamentacõn or ellys it wold hurt
her gretly[2] & pauenture put her in ieoperdy of
her lyfe. To whõ this womã ãfweryd & fayd/
I wys good gofyp I haue gret caufe to morne if
ye knew all/ for I haue byryed .iii. hufbandys befyde thys man/ but I was neuer ĩ the cafe y^t I am
now/ for there was not one of thẽ but whẽ that
I folowid the corfe to chyrch yet I was fure
alway[3] of an other hufbãd before that ye corfe[4]
cam out of my houfe/ & now I am fure of no
nother hufband & therfore ye may be fure I haue
gret caufe to be fad and heuy.

¶ By thys tale ye may fe that the olde puerbe
ys trew that yt is as gret pyte to fe a woman wepe
as a gofe to go barefote.

xi. *Of the woman that fayd her wooer came to late.*

This tale is taken from H. Bebelii, "Facetiæ, opufcula,"
s. l. & a. 4°. fign. Ggii: " De quadam muliere citiffime nu-
bente poft obitum primi viri: quidam caupo erat ad pontem
æni; vulgo Ifbruck, qui cum ad medium annum valetudinarius

[1] *to comfort*] Hazl. comfort.
[2] *hurt her gretly*] Hazl. hurt her.
[3] *I was fure alway*] Hazl. I was fure.
[4] *before that the corfe*] Hazl. before the corfe.

vitam tandem cum morte commutaffet, vxor eius funus profecuta miferabiles edebat eiulatus, obftinateque lachrymabat, adeo vt ducere eam cogeretur feruus fuus, qui eam pro virili parte confolabatur. Cum vero ipfa quereretur fe neminem habere cum quo cauponam adminiftraret (vt moris eft mulieribus multa conquerentibus) famulus fua in homines merita, qualiter quoque notus effet declarando, appellauit eam de coniugio. Illa inter eiulandum dixit. Ah nimis fero petifti, paulo enim ante alteri promifi."

Imitated in "Uncafing of Machivils Inftructions to his Sonne," 1613, fign. C, 3, and in J. W. Kirchhof, "Wendunmuth," Frankf. 1573, i. No. 346, fol. 333. Joh. Pet. de Memel, "Luftige Gefellfchaft," ed. 1695, No. 524, goes even farther, the wife was already engaged before the death of her hufband.

NOTHER woman there was that knelyd at y^e mas of requiẽ whyle the corfe of her hufbande lay on the bere in the chyrch. To whom a yonge man came to fpeke wyth her in her ere as thoughe hyt had bene for fom matre concernyng the funerallys/howe be yt he fpake of no fuch matter but only wowyd her that he myghte be her hufbande/to whome fhe anfweryde & fayde thus/ Syr by my trouthe I am fory that ye come fo late/ for I am fped all redy/ For I was made fure yefter day to a nother man.

¶ By thys tale ye may perceyue that women ofte tymes be wyfe and lothe to lofe any tyme.

XII. *Of the mylner with the golden thombe.*

See Brand's "Popular Antiquities," 1849, vol. iii. p. 387; Hazlitt's edition, p. 23, note 2, and p. 125, note to p. 23.

MERCHANT that thought to deride a myllner feyd vnto yͤ mylner fyttyng among company. Sir I haue hard fay that euery trew mylner that tollythe trewlye hath a gyldeyn thombe/ the mylner anfwered & feyd it was trewth/¹ Then quod the merchaunt I pray the let me fe thy thomb/ & when the mylner fhewyd hys thomb the merchaunt fayd I can not perceyue yᵗ thy thombe is gylt/ but yt ys but² as all other mennys thõbis be/to whom the mylner anfweryd & feyd/ Syr trothe yt ys that my thõb is gylt how be it³ ye haue no power to fe it/ for ther is a properte euer incidēt therto yᵗ he yᵗ ys a cokecold fhall neuer haue power to fe yt.

XIII. *Of the horfman of yrelond that prayd Oconer to hang vp the frere.*

A very fimilar ftory in "Neuvermehrte luftige Pennal-Poffen," s. l. & a. 8vo. fign. C, 5 *verfo*; and in Jacob Frey,

---

¹ *trewth*] Hazl. true.   ² *but it is but*] Hazl. but it is.
    ³ *how be it*] Hazl. but.

"Die Gartengefellfchaft," s. l. & a. (1556), Cap. 125, fol. 122: "Einen Dieb wolt man henken, der bat den Pfarrherrn, er folt das Nachtmahl für ihn effen," ed. Frankf. 1590, fol. 97.

ONE callyd[4] Oconer an yrifh lorde toke an horfeman pryfoner that was one of hys gret enmys/ whiche for any requeft or yntrety yt ye horfman made gaue iugement that he fhulde incōtynēt be hāgyd/ & made a frere to fhryue hym and bad hym make hym redy to dye. Thys frere yt fhroue hym examyned hym of dyuers fynes & afkyd hym amōg othere whyche were the grettyfte fynnys that euer he dyde/ thys horfeman anfweryd & fayde one of the grettyft actys that euer I dyde whyche I now moft repent is that when I toke Oconer the lafte weke in a churche and ther I myght haue brennyd hym church and all & becaufe I had confcyence & pyte of brennyng of the church I taryed ye tyme fo long yt oconer efcaped/ & that fame deferring of brennyng of the church & fo long taryeng of that tyme is one of the worft actys yt euer I dyd wherof I mofte repente/ Thys frere perceyuyng hym in that mynd fayd pece man[5] in the name of god & change yt mynde

[4] *One callyd*] Hazl. One whiche was called.
[5] *pece man*] Hazl. peace.

& dye in charite or els thou ſhalt neuer come in heuen/ nay quod the hors man I wyll neuer change yᵗ mynde what ſo euer ſhall come to my ſoule/ thys frere pceyuyng hym thys ſtyll to contynew hys mīde cā to oconer & ſeyd ſyr in yᵉ name of god haue ſome pyte vppõ thys mannys ſowle & let hym not dye now tyll he be in a better mynde/ For yf he dye now he ys ſo far out of charyte yᵗ vtterly hys ſoule ſhalle be dampnyd/ and ſhewyd hym what mynde he was in & all the hole matter as ys before ſhewyd. Thys horſman heryng yᵉ frere thys intrete for hym ſayd to oconer thys/ Oconer thou ſeeyſt well by thys mannys reporte yᵗ yf I dye now I am out of charyte & not redy to go to heuen & ſo it ys yᵗ I am now out of charyte in dede/ but thou ſeeſt well yᵗ this frere ys a good man he is now[1] well dyſpoſyd & in charyte/ and he is redy to go to heuen & ſo am not I/ therfore I pray the hang vp thys frere whyle that he hys redy to go to heuyn and lette me tary tyl a nother tyme yᵗ I may be ī charyte and redy & mete to go to heuyn. This Oconer heryng this mad anſwere of hym ſparyd the man & forgaue hym hys lyfe at that ſeaſon.

¶ By thys ye may ſe that he that is in daunger of his enmye yᵗ hath no pyte/ he can do no better

---

[1] *he is now*] Hazl. and he is now.

than² fhew to hym the vttermofte of hys malycyous mynde whych that he beryth toward hym.

XIV. *Of the preſt that ſayd nother corpus meus nor corpum meum.*

THE archdekyn of Eſſex yᵗ had bene long in auctoryte in a tyme of vyſytacion when all the preeſtys apperyd before hym callyd afyde .iii. of yᵉ yõg preſtys whych were accuſyd yᵗ they coud not well ſay theyr deuyne ſeruyce/ & aſkyd of thẽ whẽ they ſayd mas whether they ſayd corpus meus or corpũ meũ. The furſt preeſt ſayd yᵗ he ſayd corpus meus. The ſecõd ſayd yᵗ he ſayd corpũ meũ. And thẽ he aſkyd of the thyrd how he ſayd/ whych anſweryd & ſayd thus/ ſyr becauſe it is ſo gret a dout & dyuers men be in dyuers opynyons/ therfore becauſe I wold be ſure I wold not offend whẽ I come to yᵉ place I leue it clene out & ſay nothyng therfore/ wherfore he³ then openly rebukyd them all thre. But dyuers that were preſent thought more defaut in hym becauſe he hym

---

² *than*] Hazl. but.
³ *wherfore he*] Hazl. wherfore the bysſhoppe.

felfe before tyme had admyttyd them to be
preeftys.

¶ By thys tale ye may fe that one ought to
take hede how he rebukyth an other left it torne
moft to hys owne rebuke.

xv. *Of the .ii. frerys wherof the one louyd not
the ele hed nor the other the tayle.*

TWO frerys fat at a gentylmans tabyll whych had before hym õ a faftyng day an ele & cut the hed of the ele & layd it vppõ oneof yᵉ Freres trẽchars/ but the Frere becaufe he wold haue had of yᵉ myddyll part of the ele fayd to the gentylman he louyd no ele heddes/ this gentylman alfo cut the tayle of yᵉ ele & leyd it on the other Freres trẽchar/ he lykewyfe becaufe he wold haue had of the myddyll pte of yᵉ ele fayd he louyd no ele taylys. Thys gentylmã perceyuyng that: gaue the tayle to the Frere[1] yᵗ fayd he louyd not the hed/ & gaue the hed to hym that fayd he louyd not yᵉ tayle. And as for the myddell parte of the ele he ete part him felf & part he gaue to other folke at yᵉ table/ wherfore thefe freres for anger wold ete neuer a

---

[1] *to the Frere*] Hazl. to hym.

moſſell/ & ſo they for all theyr craft & ſubtylte were not onely deceyued of yᵉ beſt moſſell of yᵉ ele/ but therof had no part at al.

¶ By this ye ſe that they that couet the beſt part ſomtyme therfore loſe the meane part and all.

XVI. *Of the welchmā that ſhroue hym for brekyng his faſt on the fryday.*

This tale is found in Poggii, "Facetiæ, Opera," Baſil, 1538, fol. p. 439 : " De quodam paſtore ſimulatim conſitente : Paſtor ouium ex ea regni Neapolitani ora, quæ olim latrociniis operam dabant ſemel confeſſorem adijt, ſua peccata dicturus. Cum ad ſacerdotis genua procubuiſſet, parce mihi (inquit ille lachrimans) pater mi, quoniam grauiter deliqui. Cum juberet dicere quid eſſet. Atque ille ſæpius id verbum interaſſet, tanquam qui nepharium admiſiſſet ſalus. Tandem hortatu ſacerdotis, ait ſe cum caſeum faceret, ieiunij tempore, expreſſura lactis guttas quaſdam quas non ſpreuiſſet in os deſilijſſe. Tum ſacerdos qui mores illius patriæ noſſet ſubridens, cum dixiſſet illum delinquiſſe qui quadrageſimam non ſeruaſſet, quæſivit numquid aliis obnoxius eſſet peccatis? Abnuente paſtore, rogauit num cum alijs paſtoribus quenquam peregrinum ut mos eſſet illius regionis tranſeuntem ſpoliaſſet, aut peremiſſet? Sæpius inquit, uterque in re cum reliquis ſum verſatus. Sed iſtud ait apud nos ita eſt conſuetum, ut nulla conſcientia fiat," &c.

 WELCHMAN dwellynge in a wylde place of walys came to hys curate in the tyme of lent & was cõfeſſyd. & when his confeſſyon was in maner at the end the curate aſked him whether[1] he had any other thyng to ſay yᵗ greuyd his cõſcyẽce/ whych ſore abaſshyd anſweryd no word a gret whyle/ at laſt by exortacion of hys gooſtly fader he ſayd yᵗ there was one thyng in his mynd that gretly greuyd hys cõſciẽce which he was aſhamed to vtter/ for it was ſo greuous yᵗ he trowid god wold neuer forgyue hym/ to whom the curate ãſweryd & ſayd yᵗ goddys mercy was aboue all/ & bad hym not dyſpayre in the mercy of god/ For what ſo euer it was yf he were repentaũte yᵗ god wold forgyue hym/ And ſo by long exortacion at the laſt he ſhewyd it & ſeyd thus/ Syr it happenyd onis that as my wyfe was making a cheſe vppon a fryday I wold haue[2] ſayed whether it had ben ſalt or freſh and toke a lytyll of the whey in my hand & put it in my mouth & or I was ware part of it went downe my throte agaynſt my wyll & ſo I brake my faſt/ to whom the curate ſayd & if ther be no nother

[1] *whether*] Hazl. and.
[2] *I wold haue*] Hazl. I wolde fayne haue.

thyng I warant god ſhall forgiue the. So whã he had well comfortyd hym wᵗ yᵉ mercy of god the curate prayd hym to anſwer a queſtion & to tell hym treuth/ & when the welchman had pro-myſyd to tell the treuth/ the curate ſayd that there were robberys and murders done nye the place where he dwelt & dyuers men foũd ſlayne & aſkyd hym whether he were cõſentyng to any of them/ to whõ he anſwerid & ſayd yes & ſayd he was ptee to many of them & dyd helpe to robbe and to ſle³ dyuers of them. Then the curate aſkyd hym why he dyd not cõfeſſe him therof/ the welch man ãſweryd & ſayd he toke yᵗ for no ſynne for it was a cuſtome amonge them yᵗ whan any boty came of any rych merchaunt rydyng yᵗ it was but a good neybours dede one to help a nother when one callyd a nother/ & ſo they toke that but for good felyſhyp & ney-bourhod.

¶ Here ye may⁴ ſe yᵗ ſome haue remorſe of conſcyence of ſmall venyall ſinys & fere not to do gret offencys wᵗout ſhame of yᵉ world or drede of god : & as yᵉ cõen puerb is they ſtũble at a ſtraw & lepe ouer a blok.

³ *to ſle*] Orig. reads toſle.
⁴ *ye may*] Hazl. maye ye.

XVII. *Of the merchaūt of lōdō that put nobles ĩ his mouth ĩ his deth bed.*

RYCH couetous marchāte ther was yᵗ dwellyd in Lōdon whych euer gaderyd money & coud neuer fynd in hys hert to fpend noght¹ vppon hym felf nor vppon no mā els/ whych fell fore fyk/ & as he lay on hys deth bed had hys purs lyeng at his beddys hed/ & had fuche a loue to hys money that he put his hand in his purs & toke out therof .x. or .xii. li ĩ nobles & put them in his mouth/ And becaufe his wyfe and other pceyuyd him very fyk and lyke to dye they exortyd hym to be confeffyd and brought yᵉ curate vnto him/ whych when they had caufyd hym to fey Benedicite yᵉ curat bad hym cry god mercy & fhew his fynnys.² Than this fyk man began to fey I cry god mercy I haue offendyd in yᵉ .vij. dedly fynnys & broken the .x. comaundementys/ & becaufe of the gold in hys mouth he mufflede fo in hys fpeche that the curate cowde not well vnderftande hym/ wherefore the curate afked hym what he hadde in hys mouthe that letted hys fpeche/ I wys maftere perfone quod the fyk man muffelynge

¹ *noght*] Hazl. ought.
² *fhew his fynnys*] Hazl. fhewe to hym.

I haue nothyng in my mouth but a lyttyll money becaufe I wot not whether I fhall go I thoughte I wolde take fome fpendyng money wyth me for I wot not what nede I fhall haue therof/ And incontynent after that feyynge dyed before he was confeffed or repentant that ony man could perceue/ and fo by lykelyhode went to the deuyll.

¶ By thys tale ye may fe that they that all theyre lyuys wylle neuer do charyte to theyr neyghbours/ that god in tyme of theyr dethe wyll not fuffer them to haue grace of repentaunce.

XVIII. *Of the mylner that ftale the nuttys & of the tayler that ftale a fhepe.*

The fource of this tale is perhaps the fabliau Etula, in Legrand d'Auffy, " Fabliaux," tom. iii. p. 77; better in Sinner, " Catalogus Codicum MSS." tom. iii. p. 379, No. 14. It is alfo related in the " Scala Celi (liber ifte vocatur Scala Celi, Ulme, Joh. Zainer, 1480, fol.), de furto, quinto," fol. 101 verfo: " Legitur quod cum duo latrones conveniffent ut furarentur nuces et alter carnes; perveniens ad fores ecclefiæ qui furatus fuerat nuces incepit frangere et comedere eas ibi. Cujus fonitum audiens ille, qui cuftodiebat ecclefiam, credens, quod dæmon ingreffus eft clauftrum et cuidam claudo, qui ire non potuit et forti

rustico videnti nunciavit. Et dum ingreſſi fuiſſent eccle-
ſiam, latro comedebat nuces, credens quod eſſet ſocius ſuus,
qui portaret arietem, incepit clamare: Eſtne bene pinguis
quem portas? Tunc ruſticus territus qui portabat claudum,
credens quod eſſet dæmon: Neſcio ſi eſt pinguis vel macer,
ſed nunc relinquo eum vobis. Et projecto claudo ad ter-
ram tibiam aliam ſibi frigit." Alſo in Joh. de Bromyard,
"Summa prædicantium," Litt. O, ii. § 6.

Imitations are: J. Pauli, "Schimpff und Ernſt," Straſſ-
burg, 1535, fol. No. 76, fol. 15; G. Wickram, "Der
Rollwagen," s. l. 1557, No. 67, (Frankf. 1590, fol. 72:
"Wie zween Dieb einem Pfaffen das Podagram vertri-
ben"), reprinted in Wackernagel, "Deutſches Leſebuch,"
Wickram; Hans Sachs, "Gedichte," vol. ii. l. 4, fol. 73,
Nürnberg, 1591, fol.: "Die zwen diebiſchen Bachanten
in dem Toden Kercker."

HERE was a certayn ryche huſband-
man in a vyllage whych loued nottes
merueluoſly well & ſet trees of filberdys
& other nut trees in his orchard/ & noriſhid
them well all hys lyfe/ & when he dyed he made
hys executours to make promiſe to bery wᵗ hym
yn hys graue a bage of nottis or els they ſholde
not be hys executours/ which executours for
fere of loſyng theyre[1] romys fulfyllyd hys wyll[2]
& dyd ſo. It happenyd yᵗ the ſame nyght after
that he was beryed there was a mylnere in a

---

[1] *of loſyng theyre*] Hazl. of leſynge of theyre.
[2] *wyll*] Hazl. mynde.

whyte cote came to this mays garden to thetet³
to ſtele a bag of nottis/ & in yᵉ way he met
wᵗ a tayler in a blak cote an vnthrift of hys
accoyntaūce & ſhewyd hym hys intent/ This
tayler lykewyſe ſhewyd hym yᵗ he intēdyd yᵉ
ſame tyme to ſtele a ſhepe/ & ſo they both there
agreyd to go forthward euery man ſeuerally
wᵗ hys purpoſe & after yᵗ they apoynted to make
good chere ech wᵗ other & to mete agayne in yᵉ
chyrch porch/ & he that came furſt to tary for
the other.

This mylner when he had ſpede of hys nottis
came furſt to the chyrch porche & there taryed
for hys felowe and the mene whyle ſatte ſtyll
there & knakked nottys.

It fortuned than the ſexten of the church becauſe yt was abowt .ix. of the clok cam to ryng
curfu.⁴ & when he lokyd in yᵉ porch & ſaw one
all in whyte knakkyng nottes/ he had went⁵ it
had bene yᵉ dede man ryſen owt of hys graue
knakkynge yᵉ nottes yᵗ wer byryed wᵗ hym &
ran home agayn in all haſt and tolde to a krepyll
yᵗ was in hys howſe what he had ſene. This
crepyll thus heryng⁶ rebukyd yᵉ ſexten & ſeyd yᵗ

---

³ *to thentent*] i. e. to the entent.
⁴ *curfu*] i. e. evening-bell.
⁵ *went*] i. e. weened.
⁶ *thus heryng*] Hazl. thus herynge hym.

yf he were able to go he wold go thyder & cōiure yͤ fprite/ by my trouth quod yͤ fexten & yf thou darſt do yᵗ I wyl bere the on my nek & fo they both agreed. The fexten toke yͤ crepul on hys nek & cam in to yͤ chyrchyard agayn/ & yͤ mylner in yͤ porch faw one comyng bering a thing on his bak had went it had ben yͤ taylour cōmyng wᵗ the fhepe & rofe vp to mete thẽ/ & as he cam towarde thẽ he afkeyd & feyd/ Is he fat/ is he fat/ yͤ fexten heryng hym fey fo/ for fere caſt the crepull down & feyd fat or lene take hym ther for me/[1] and ran away/ & the creple by myracle was made hole & rã away as faſt as he or faſter/ This mylner perceyuing yᵗ they were .ii.[2] & yᵗ one ran after a nother fuppofyng[3] yᵗ one had fpyed yͤ tayler ſtelyng yͤ fhepe & yᵗ he had ron after hym to haue taken hym/ and fered yᵗ fom body alfo had fpyed hym ſtelyng nottes[4] he for fere left hys nottes behynd hym and as fecretly as he cowde ran home to hys myll/ And anon after yᵗ he was gon yͤ tayler cam wᵗ the ſtolyn fhepe vppon hys nek to the chyrch porch[5] to

---

[1] *ther for me*] Hazl. as he is.
[2] *.ii.*] Hazl. two.   [3] *fuppofyng*] Hazl. thoughte.
[4] *and fered that fom body alfo had fpyed hym ſtelyng nottes*] Hazl. and fearyng that one had fpyed hym alfo ſtelynge the nuttes.
[5] *chyrch porch*] Hazl. churche.

feke the mylner & when he fownd ther the not
fhalys he fuppofyd y^t hys felow had be ther and
gone home as he was in dede/ wherefore he toke
vp ye fhepe agayne on hys nek and went[6] to
ward the myl/ But yet duryng this whyle the
fextē which ran away went not to hys owne
houfe but wēt to the pyfh pryftis chāber/ &
fhewd hym how the fpryte of ye man was ryfē
out of hys graue knakkīg nottes as ye haue
hard before/ wherfor ye preft fayd that he wold
go cōiure hym yf the fexten wold go w^t hym/
& fo they both agreed/ ye preft dyd on hys furples
& a ftole about hys nek & toke holy water w^t
hym and cam w^t the fextē toward ye church/ &
as fone as he enteryd in to[7] ye church yarde, The
tayler w^t the whyte fhepe on hys nek intendyng
as I before haue fhewid yow to go down to y^e
myll met w^t them & had went y^t ye preft in hys
furples had ben ye mylner in hys whyte cote/ &
feyd to hym by god I haue hym I haue hym
meanyng by[8] the fhepe y^t he had ftolyn/ the preft
perceyuynge the tayler all in blak & a whyte thyng
on hys nek had went it had ben ye deuyll beryng
away the fpryte of ye dede man y^t was beryed
& ran away as fafte as he coud takyng ye way
downe toward the myll/ & ye fexten ronnyng

[6] *and went*] Hazl. went.   [7] *in to*] Hazl. in.
[8] *by*] i. e. thereby.

after hĩ. This tayler feyng one folowyng hĩ had went yᵗ one had folowed the mylner to haue don hym fome hurt & thought he wold folow if nede were to help yᵉ mylner. & went forth tyl he cam to the myll & knokked at yᵉ myldore/ yᵉ mylner beyng w'yn afked who was ther yᵉ tayler ãfwerd & faid by god I haue caught one of them & made hĩ fure & tyed hym faft by yᵉ leggys menynge by the fhepe yᵗ he had ftolen & had thẽ on hys nek tyed faft by the leggys.¹ But yᵉ mylner heryng hym fey yᵗ he had hym tyed faft by the leggys had wente it had bẽ the conftable yᵗ had takẽ the tayler for ftelyng of the fhepe & had tyed him by the leggys/ & ferid yᵗ he had comen to haue taken hym alfo for ftelyng of the nottys/ wherfore the mylner openyd a bak dore & ran away as faft as he coud. The taylour heryng the bak dore openyng wẽt on yᵉ other fyde of yᵉ myll/ & there faw the mylner ronnyng away/ & ftode there a littyll whyle mufyng wᵗ yᵉ fhepe on his nek. Then was the paryfh preeft & the fextẽ ftandyng there vnder the mylhoufe hydyng them for fere & faw the taylour agayn wᵗ yᵉ fhepe on his nek had wend ftyll it had bene the dyuyll wᵗ the fpryt of the dede man on hys nek & for fere ran away/ but becaufe they knew not

¹ *menynge by the fhepe . . . by the leggys.*] Wanting in Hazl.

the ground well/ the preeſt lepte into a dyche almoſt ouer the hed lyke to be drounyd that he cryed wyth a loud voyce help help. Then the taylour lokyd about & ſaw the mylner roñe away & the ſexten a nother way & hard the preeſt cry help: had wend it had bene the cõſtable wᵗ a gret cõpany cryeng for help to take hym & to bryng hym to pryſon for ſtelyng of yᵉ ſhepe wherfore he threw downe the ſhepe & ran away a nother way as faſte as he coud/ & ſo euery man was afferd of other wythout cauſe.

¶ By thys ye may ſe well it is foly for any man to fere a thyng to mych tyll that he ſe ſome proue or cauſe.

XIX. Of the .iiii. elem̄etys where they ſhulde ſone be found.

A ſubſtantially ſimilar ſtory occurs in " Tre hundrede udvalgte hiſtorier, &c." 4th edit. Copenh. 1781, p. 19⁸ (a tranſlation of Pauli's " Schimpff und Ernſt"); reprinted in R. Nyerup, " Almindelig Morſkabs laeſning," Copenh. 1816, p. 254. Alſo in H. Sachs, " Gedichte," buch i. thiel 3, Nüremberg, 1558, fol. f. 255: " Ein geſprech der vier Element mit Fraw Warheit."

N yᵉ old world when all thyng coud ſpeke yᵉ .iiii. elementys met togeder for many thyngys whych they had to

do becaufe they muft medyll alway one with a nother: & had cōmunicaciō to geder of dyuers matters/ & becaufe they coud not conclude all theyr maters at y^t feafon they appoyntyd to breke comunycacyon for y^t tyme & to mete agayn a nother tyme/ therfore ech one of thē fhewyd to other wher theyre moft abydyng was & where theyr felows fhuld fynd them if nede fhuld requyre: & furft ye yerth fayd brethern ye know well as for me I am pmanēt alway & not remouable therfor ye may be fure to haue me alway whan ye lyft. The water feyd yf ye lyfte to feke me ye fhalbe fure euer[1] to haue me vnder a toft of grene rufhys or ellys in a womans eye. The wynde fayd yf ye lyft to feke me[2] ye fhalbe fure euer to haue me amonge afpyn leuys or els in a womans tong. Then quod the fyre yf any of you lyft to feke me: ye fhall euer[3] be fure to fynd me in a flynt ftone or els in a womans hart.

¶ By thys tale ye may lerne afwell the propertes of y^e .iiii. elementys as ther properte[4] of a woman.

[1] *euer*] wanting in Hazl.
[2] *to feke me*] Hazl. to fpeke wyth me.
[3] *euer*] wanting in Hazl.
[4] *properte*] Hazl. properte is.

xx. *Of the woman that powryd the potage in the Tuggys male.*

THERE was a iuſtyce but late in yᵉ realme of englond called maſter Uauyſour a very homly man & rude of condycions & louyd neuer to ſpēd mych money/ This maſter Uauyſour rode on a tyme in hys cyrcute in a place of the north cōtrey[5] where he had agreed wᵗ the ſhyryf for a certayn ſome of money for hys chargys thorowe the ſhyre/ ſo that at euery Inne & lodgyng thys maſter vaueſour payd for hys own coſtys. It fortunyd ſo yᵗ when he cam to a certayn lodgyng he cōmaunded one Torpyn hys ſeruāt to ſe yᵗ he vſed good huſbondry[6] & to ſaue ſuche thynges as were laft & to cary it wᵗ hym to ſerue hym at the next baytyng. Thys Torpyn doyng hys maſters cōmaūdemēt toke yᵉ brokyn brede brokyn mete & all ſych thīg yᵗ was laft & put it in hys male/[7] The wyfe of yᵉ houſe pceyuyng yᵗ he toke all ſuche fragmentys & vytayle wᵗ hym yᵗ was laft

[5] *in a place of the north contrey*] Hazl. in the northe contrey.

[6] *huſbondry*] i. e. economy.

[7] *in hys mayle*] Hazl. in his mayſters cloth ſak. [Hazl. has *cloth ſak* for *male* throughout the whole tale.]

& put it in hys male/[1] fhe brought vp y^t podege y^t was laft ĩ the pot & when torpyn had torned hys bak a lytyll fyde[2] fhe pouryd ye podege in to ye male whych ran vpon hys robe of fkarlet & other hys garmẽtys & rayed[3] them very euyll that they were mych hurt therw^t. Thys Torpyn fodeynly tornyd him & faw it/ reuylyd the wyfe therfor & ran to hys mafter & told hym what fhe had don/ wherfor mafter Uauefour incõtinẽt callyd ye wyfe & feyd to her thus. Thou drab quod he what haft thou dõ why haft thou pouryd ye podege in my male & marryd my raymẽt & gere/ O fyr quod ye wyfe I know well ye ar a iudge of ye realme/ & I perceyue by you : your mĩd is to do ryght & to haue that that is[4] your owne/ & your mynd is to haue all thyng w^t you y^t ye haue payd for/ both brokyn brede mete[5] & other thynges y^t is left : & fo it is reafon that ye haue/ & therfore becaufe your feruant hath taken the brede & the mete[6] & put it ĩ your male I haue therfore put in your male[7] the podege y^t be laft becaufe ye haue well & truly payd for them

---

[1] *hys male*] Hazl. the cloth fake.
[2] *fyde*] Hazl. afyde.   [3] *rayed*] i. e. defiled.
[4] *that that is*] Hazl. that is.
[5] *brokyn brede mete*] Hazl. broken mete.
[6] *the brede and the mete*] Hazl. the broken mete.
[7] *therfore put in your male*] Hazl. therin put.

for yf[8] I fhuld kepe ony thyng from you y^t ye haue payd for: peraduenture ye wold troble me in the law an other tyme.

¶ Here ye may fe y^t he y^t playth the nygarde to mych fometyme yt torneth hym to hys owne loffe.

XXI. *Of the weddyd men that cam to heuyn to clayme theyr herytage.*

A correfponding tale in Fernan Caballero, "Elia, ó la Efpaña treinta años ha," Madrid, 1857, page 93. (Tranflated into German by H. Wolf, Paderborn, 1860, p. 116.)

A CERTAYNE weddyd man there was whyche whan he was dede cã to heuen gatys to faynt Peter & fayd he cã to claym his herytage[9] which he had deferuyd. Saynt Peter afkyd hym what he was/ & he fayd a weddyd mã/ anon Seynt peter openyd ye gatys & bad hym come in[10] & fayd he was worthy to haue hys herytage becaufe he had had much trobyll & was worthy to haue a crowne of glory. Anon after y^t there cam a nother man that claymyd

---

[8] *for yf*] Hazl. Yf.
[9] *his herytage*] Hazl. hys bad heretage.
[10] *come in*] Hazl. to come in.

heuyn/ & fayd to Seynt Peter he had had .ii. wyuys/ to whom Seynt peter āfweryd and fayd come in for thou art worthy to haue a doble crown of glory/ for thou haft had doble troble/ at ye laft there cam a thyrd[1] claymyng heuen & fayd to Saynt peter that he had had .iii. wyuys & defyryd to come in/ what quod Seynte Peter thou haft bene onys in troble & therof delyueryd/ and then wyllyngly woldyft be trobyld agayn & yet agayn therof delyueryd/ & for all y^t couldeft[2] not beware ye thyrde tyme/ but entereft wyllyngely in trobyll agayne therefore go thy way to hell for thou fhalte neuer come in heuen for thou arte not worthy.

¶ Thys tale is a warnyng to them that haue[3] bene twyfe in parell to beware how they come therin the thyrd tyme.

.

XXII. *Of the merchaunte that chargyd hys fonne to fynde one to fynge for hys fowle.*

This ftory originates in Joh. de Bromyard, "Summa Prædicantium," Litt. E, viii. § 17: " Sicut patet de illo qui moriens, vxore executrice facta: bouem pro anima fua legauit vt fertur, vxor vero bouem et gallum fimul ad forum

---

[1] *a thyrd*] Hazl. the thyrd. [2] *couldeft*] Hazl. coulde.
[3] *haue*] in orig. houe.

ducens: utrumque fimul vendidit hac conuentione: quod emptor pro gallo marcam anglicanam et pro boue obolum daret, quod cum factum fuiffet: obolum pro anima dedit marito." The fame ftory in Ropertus Holkot, "Super Libros Sapientiæ," Reutlingen, 1489, fol. 111. Imitated in Pauli, "Schimpff und Ernft," Strasfburg, 1535, No. 438, fol. 71; in Gerlach, "Eutrapeliarum libri III." Lips. 1656, lib. i. No. 656, p. 157; in J. P. de Memel, "Luftige Gefellfchaft," ed. 1695, No. 622, p. 263; and in "Ein reicher Vorrath Anmuthiger Ergoetzlichkeiten," ed. 1702, No. 142, p. 94.

A RYCH merchant of london there was which had but one fonne yt was fomewhat vnthryfty therefore his fader vppon hys deth bed called hym to hym & feyd he knew well yt he had ben vnthrifty howbeit yf he knew he wold amend hys condiciõs he wolde make hym his executoure & leue hym his goodys fo yt he wold promyfe[4] to praye for his fowle: & to fynde[5] one dayly to fyng for hym/ whyche thyng to performe hys fon there made a faythfull promyfe. After yt thys mã made hym hys executoure & dyed/ But after that hys foñe kept fuch ryot yt in fhort tyme he had wafted & fpend all & had nothynge left but a hen & a cok that was hys faders. It fortunyd than that one of hys

[4] *promyfe*] Hazl. promyfe him.
[5] *& to fynde*] Hazl. and fo fynde.

Frendys came to hym & fayd he was fory y' he had waftyd fo mych & afkyde hym how he wolde pform hys pmyfe made to hys father y' he wold kepe one to fing for him.

Thys yong man ãfweryd & fayd by god yet I wyll performe my promyfe/ for I wyll kepe thys fame cok alyue ftyll and he wyll krowe euery daye and fo he fhall fynge euery day for my faders fowle/ & fo I wyll performe my promyfe well ynough.

¶ By thys ye may fe that it is wyfdome for a man to do good[1] dedys hym felf whyle he is here & not to truft to the prayer and promys of hys executours.

XXIII. *Of the mayd wafhyng clothys and anfwered the frere.*

THERE was a mayde ftode by a ryuers fyde in her fmok wafhynge clothys. And as fhe ftoupyd oft tymys in her fmokke[2] cleuyd betwene her butokkes/ By whome there came a frere feynge her and fayde in fport. Mayd mayde take hede for Bayard bytys on the

---

[1] *good*] orig. reads goodys.
[2] *oft tymys in her fmokke*] Hazl. ofttymes, her fmocke.

brydyll. Nay wys mafter frere quod the mayden he doth but wype hys mouth and wenyth ye wyll come & kyffe hym.

¶ By thys ye may fe that a womans[3] anfwer is neuer to feke.

XXIV. Of the .iii. wyfe men of gotam.

The fame ftory in "Merie Tales of the Mad Men of Gotam." The firft tale in "Shakefpeare Jeft Books," iii. p. 4.

A CERTAYN man there was dwellynge in a towne callyd Gotam which went to a fayre .iii. myle of[4] to by fhepe/ & as he cam ouer a brydge he met w^t one of hys neybours & told him whether he went/ & he afkyd hym whych way he wold bryng thẽ/ whych fayd he wold brĩg thẽ ouer the fame brydge/ nay quod the other mã but thou fhalt not/ by god quod he but I wyll/ ye other agayn faid he fhuld not/ & he agayn faid he wold bryng them ouer fpyte of his teth & fo fell at wordys/ & at the laft to buffertys that eche one knokkyd other well about the heddys w^t theyre fyftys. To

---

[3] *a womans*] Hazl. womans.
[4] *iii. myle of*] Hazl. iii. myle for.

whom there cam a thyrd man which was a mylner wyth a fak of mele vppõ a horfe a neybour of theyrs & partyd them &[1] afkyd thẽ what was the caufe of theyr varyaunce/ whych then fhewyd hym the matter & caufe as ye haue harde/ Thys thyrd man the mylner thought to rebuke[2] theyr folyfhnes with[3] a famylyer example & toke hys fak of mele from his hors bak & openyd it & pouryd all the mele in the fak ouer the bridge into the ronyng riuer wherby all the mele was loft & fayd thus. By my trouth neybors becaufe ye ftryue for dryuyng ouer the brydge thofe fhepe which be not yet bought nor wot not wher they be/ me thynkyth therfore there is euyn as mych wyt in your heddys as there is mele[4] in my fak.

¶ Thys tale fhewyth you that fome man takyth vppõ hym to fhew other men wyfdome when he is but a fole hym felf.

[1] *partyd them &*] Hazl. paciently.
[2] *to rebuke*] Hazl. for to rebuke.
[3] *theyr folyfhnes with*] Hazl. them by.
[4] *is mele*] Hazl. is mele now.

MERY TALYS. 47

xxv. *Of the gray frere that anſweryd his penytent.*

A correſponding tale, ſee in J. Frey, " Die Garten-geſellſchaft," s. l. & a, cap. 30, fol. 36 verſo: " Von einem Landſknecht, der einem alten Münch beichtet," ed. Frankf. 1590, fol. 29 *verſo*.

MAN there was[5] that came to confeſſe hym ſelf[6] to a gray frere & ſhroue him that he had layne with a yong gentil-womā/ yᵉ frere than aſkyd hym in what place/ & he ſaid it was in a goodly chāber all nyght lōg in a ſofte warme bed/ The frere heryng that ſhruggyd in hys clothys & ſayd/ now by ſwete ſeynt fraunces then waſt thou verye well at eaſe.

xxvi. *Of the gentylman that bare the ſege borde on his nek.*

CHANDELER beīg a wydower dwel-lig at holborne brige in lōdō had a fayre doughter/ whom a yōg gentyl-man of dauys Inne woyd gretly[7] to haue hys plea-ſure of her/ whych by long ſute to her made at

[5] *there was*] orig. reads there man.
[6] *hym ſelf*] Hazl. hym.   [7] *gretly*] Hazl. ſore.

yᵉ laſt graūtyd him & poyntyd hym to cõe vppõ a night to her faders houſe in yᵉ euenyng & ſhe wold conuey him into her chāber ſecretly whych was an inner chamber wythin her faders chāber/ ſo accordīg to yᵉ poītmēt all thīg was pformyd So yᵗ he lay wᵗ her all nyght & made good chere tyll about .iiii.¹ a clok ī yᵉ mornīg/ at which time it fortunyd this yõg gētylmā fell a coughīg/ whych cā vppõ hym ſo ſore yᵗ he coud not refrayn. Thys yong wench² then fering her fader that lay in the next chaūber bad hym go put hys hed in the draught left yᵗ her fader ſhuld here him : which after her councell roſe in hys ſhyrt & ſo dyd/ but thē becauſe of the ſauor of the draught it cauſyd hym to cough mich more & louder that yᵉ wēchis fader hard hym³ & aſkyd of hys doughter what man was that yᵗ coughid⁴ ī her chāber/ ſhe anſweryd & ſayd no body. But euer thys yõg mā coughid ſtyll more & more whom the fader heryng ſeyd/ by goddys body here thou lyeſt I wyll ſe who hys there & roſe out of hys bed.

Thys wench perceyuyng⁵ her fader ryſyng cam

¹ .iiii.] Hazl. foure.
² *Thys yong wench*] Hazl. Thys wench.
³ *hard hym*] Hazl. herde it.
⁴ *what man was that that coughid*] Hazl. what man it was that coughed.
⁵ *perceyuyng*] Hazl. perceyued.

to the gentylmā & ſayd take hede ſyr to your ſelf my fader comyth.⁶ Thys gentylman ſodēly therwyth abaſhyd wolde haue pullyd hys hed out of the drawght hole whych was very ſtreyte for hys hed that he pullyd the ſege bord vp therwyth/ & hangyng about hys nek ran vppon the fader beyng an old man & gaue hym a gret fall/ & bare hym down & hurt hys arme/ & openyd the dorys & rā into yᵉ ſtrete wyth yᵉ draught borde about hys nek toward dauys Inne as faſt as he coud.

This wēch for fere rā out of her faders houſe & cā not there a moneth after. Thys gentylman as he ran vppon holborne brydge met wᵗ a colyers cart laden wᵗ colys where there was .ii. or .iii.⁷ ſkyttyſh horſys/ which when they ſaw thys gentylman rōnyng ſtart aſyde & threw down yᵉ cart wyth colys/ & drew it aſyde & brake yᵉ cart rope/ wherby the colys fell out ſome in one place ſome in an other/ & after the horſys brake theyr traſys & ran ſome toward ſmythfeld. & ſome toward newgate that the colyer rā after them & was ā howre & more or he coud get his horſe to geder agayn/ By whych tyme the people of the ſtrete were ryſen and cā to yᵉ ſtrete & ſaw yt ſtrawyd wyth colys euery one for hys part gaderyd vp the

---

⁶ *my fader comyth*] Hazl. for my fader comyth.
⁷ *.ii. or .iii.*] Hazl. two or thre.

colys : that ye moſt part of the colys were gone or the colyer had got hys horſys.

But duryng thys whyle the gẽtylman wẽt thorow ſeynt andrews chyrchyard toward dauys Inne/ & there met wyth the ſextẽ comyng to church[1] to rĩg to morow mas : whych when he ſaw the gentylman in the churchyarde in hys ſhyrt w^t the draght bord about hys nek/ had wẽd it had ben a ſpryt : & cryed alas alas a ſpryt & ran bak agayn to hys houſe almoſt at ye barrys & for fere was almoſt out of hys wyt y^t he was ye worſe halfe a yere after.

Thys gentlman than becauſe dauys Inne gatys were not open went on the bak ſyde & lept ouer the garden wall/ but in lepyng the ſege bord[2] ſo trobled hym that[3] he fell down in to the garden & had almoſt brokẽ his nek & there ley[4] ſtyll tyll y the prĩcipall cam in to the gardyn/ whych when he ſaw hym ly there had wend ſom man had be ſlayne & there caſt ouer ye wall & durſt not come nye him tyll he had callyd vp hys company/ whych when many of the gentylmen wher come to gether/ lokyd well vppõ him and knew hym & after releuyd hym/ But the borde

---

[1] *comyng to church*] Hazl. commynge to attend.
[2] *ſege bord*] Hazl. draught-bord.
[3] *that*] in orig. thot.
  there ley] Hazl. there he lay.

yᵗ was about hys nek cauſyd his hed ſo to ſwell that they coud not get it of tyll they were fayne⁵ to cutte it of with hatchettys. Thus was the wench well Japyd/⁶ & for fere ſhe ran frõ her fader/ her faders arme was hurt the colyar loſt his colys the ſextẽ was almoſt out of his wyt/ & the gentylman had almoſt broke his nek.

XXVII. *Of the marchaũtys wyfe that ſeyd ſhe wolde take a nap at ſermon.*⁷

To take a nap at ſermon or at church is quite a common ſaying in Germany, ſo common, indeed, that a technical term "Kirchenſchlaf" has been given to this particular kind of nap.

A MARCHANTYS wyfe ther was in bowe paryſh in london ſome what ſtept⁸ in age to whõ her mayd cam on a ſonday in lent after dyner & ſayd/ mayſtres quod ſhe they ryng at ſeynt Thomas of acres for ther ſhall be a ſermõ prechyd anon/ to whom the mayſtres anſwerd & ſayd mary goddys blyſſyng on thy hart⁹ for warnyng me therof & becauſe I ſlept

⁵ *fayne*] Hazl. mynded.
⁶ *Japyd*] i. e. mocked.
⁷ *at ſermon*] Hazl. at a ſermon.
⁸ *ſtept*] Hazl. ſlepte.
⁹ *on thy hart*] Hazl. haue thy harte.

not well all this night I pray the brynge my
ſtole with me for I wyll go thyder to loke
wether I can take a nap there whyle the preſt
is prechyng.

¶ By this ye may ſe that many on goth to
churche as moche for other thyngys as for de-
uocyon.

XXVIII. *Of the woman that ſeyd & ſhe lyffyd a
nother yere ſhe wolde haue a kokoldis hat of her
owne.*

Too imperfect to decipher in Hazl.

THER was a certayn company of women
gatheryd to geder in cõmunycacion one
happenyd thus to ſay her pyggys after
they were farowyd dyed and wolde not lyue and
one olde wyfe of her accoyntance heryng her ſay
ſo bad her get a cockoldys Hat and put the pyggys
therin a whyle after they were farrowyd and they
ſholde lyue/ whych wyfe intendyng to do after
her counſell came to one of her goſſyppys and
ſhewyd her what medecyne was taught[1] her for
her pyggys & prayd her to lend her her huſbandys
hat/ whych anſweryd her angerly and ſayd I wold

---

[1] *taught*] orig. reads thaugh.

thou knewyſt it Drabbe I haue none for my huſbande is no cookold for I am a good woman and
ſo lyke wyfe euery wyfe anſweryd her in lyke
maner that ſhe departyd frome many of them in
anger and ſkoldynge/ But whan ſhe ſawe ſhe
coude get none ſhe came agayne to her goſſyppys
all angerly and ſayd I haue gone round aboute to
borrow a cookoldys hat and I can get none
wherefore yf I lyue another yere I wyll haue
one of myn own and be out of my neyghbours
daunger.

¶ By this tale a man may lerne that it is more
wyſdome for a man to truſt more to his owne
ſtore than to his neyghbours gentylnes.

XXIX. *Of the gentylman that wyſhyd his toth in
the gentylwomans tayle.*

A GENTYLMAN & a gentylwoman
ſat togeder talkyn whiche gentylman
had gret payn in one of his teth. &
hapnyd to ſay to the gētylwoman[2] thus. I wys
maſtres I haue a toth ī my hed which greuyth
me very ſore wherfore I wold yt were in your
tayle. She heryng hym ſaying ſo. anſweryd thus

[2] *gentylwoman*] in orig. gentylwomau.

In good fayth fyr if your toth were in my tale it coud do yt but lytyll good/ but if there be any thynge in my tale that can do your toth good I wold yt were in your toth.

¶ By this ye may fe that a womans anfwer is feldome to feke.

xxx. *Of the welchman that confeffyd hym how he had flayn a frere.*

IN the tyme of lent a welchman cam to be confeffyd of hys curat whych in hys cõfeffyon fayd that he had kyllyd a frere/ to whõ the curat fayd he coude not affoyle hym/ yet quod the welchmã yf thou kneweft all thou woldeft affoyle me well enough/ & when the curat cõmandyd hym to fhew hym all the cafe he fayd thus/ mary ther wer ii freres & I might haue flayn them both yf I had lyft but I let one fkape therfore mafter curat fet the tone agaynft the tother & then the offence ys not fo great but ye may affoyle me well ynough.

¶ By this ye may fe that dyuers menne haue fo euyll & large cõfcyens that they thynke yf they do one good dede or refrayne from the doynge[1]

---

[1] *from the doynge*] Hazl. from doynge.

of one euyll fynne that yt ys a fatysfaccyon[2] for other fynnis and offencys.

XXXI. *Of the welchman that cowde not get but a lytyll male.*

THERE was a company of gẽtylmen in northãtonſhyre whych went to hunte for deere in the porlews in the gollet befyde ſtony ſtratford/ Among which gentylmen ther was one which had a walche man to his fyruaunte a good archer/ whiche when they came to a place where they thought they ſhold haue game/ they made a ſtondyng and poyntyd thys welchman to ſtand by a tre nygh the hye way and bad hym in any wyſe to take hede that he ſhot at no[3] raſkall[4] nor medle nat without it were a male & yf it were a male to ſpare not/ wel quod this welchman let me alone. And whan this walchman had ſtande there a whyle he ſawe moche dere cõmynge/ as well of Auntelere as of Raſcall/ but eur he let them go and toke no hede to theym.

[2] *a ſatysfaccyon*] Hazl. ſatysfaccyon.
[3] *to take hede that he ſhot at no*] Hazl. to ſhote at no.
[4] *raſkall*] i.e. lean beaſt.

And within an howre after he saw come rydyng in the hye way a man of the countrey which had a boget hangynge at hys sadyll bowe. And whan this walche man had espyed hym he bad hym stand & began to drawe his bow and bad hym deliuer that lyttyll male that hynge at his sadell bowe/ Thys man for fere of hys lyfe was glad to delyuer hym his boget/ & so dyd & than rode his way & was glad he was so eskapyd. And whan this man of the countrey was gon thys welchman was very glad & went incontynent to seke his master & at last[1] founde[2] hym with his company/ and whã he sawe hym he come to hym & sayd thus/ Master by cottys plut & her nayle I haue stande yonder thys two howrys and I cowd se neuer a male but a lytell male that a man had hangyng at his sadell bow/ & that I haue gotten/ & lo here it is/ and toke his master the boget whych he had taken awey from the forsayd man/ for the whyche dede bothe the master & the seruant were afterwarde in great trouble.

¶ By thys ye may lerne yt ys gret foly for a master to put a seruant to that besynes wherof he can nothing skyll[3] and wherin he hath nat be vsyd.

[1] *at last*] Hazl. at the laste.   [2] *founde*] in orig. fonude.
[3] *skyll*] i. e. know, signify.

XXXII. *Of the gentyll woman that fayd to a gentylman ye haue a berde a boue & none benethe.*

 YONGE gentylman of the age of .xx. yere fome whate dyfpofyd to myrth and game[4] on a tyme talkyd with a gentylwoman[5] which was ryght wyfe and alfo mery. this gentyll woman as fhe talkyd with hym happenyd to loke vppon hys berde/ whiche was but yong and growen fome what[6] vppon the ouer lyppe and but lyttyll growen beneth as all[7] yonge mennys berdys cõmonly vfe to growe fayd[8] to hym thus. Syr ye haue a berde aboue and none beneth. and he herynge her fay fo/ fayd in fporte/ maftres ye haue a berde benethe and none aboue/ mary quod fhe/ then fet the tone agaynft the tother/ which anfwere made the gentylman fo abafhyd that he had not one worde to anfwer.

[4] *game*] Hazl. gaye.
[5] *gentylwoman*] orig. reads geutylwoman.
[6] *growen fome what*] Hazl. fomewhat growen.
[7] *as all*] Hazl. as all other.
[8] *fayd*] Hazl. and fayd.

XXXIII. *Of the frere that fayd our lord fed .v. M.*[1]
peple with .ij.[2] *fyſhys.*

THERE was a certayn white frere which was a very glotton and a great nyggyn whyche had an vngracyouſe boy that euer folowyd hym and bare hys cloke/ and what for the frerys[3] glottony & for his chorlyſhnes the boy where he went coude ſkant get mete inough for the frere wolde eet almoſte all hym ſelfe. But on a tyme the frere made a ſermon in the cõtrey wherin he touchyde very many myracles whiche cryſt dyd afore his paſſyon amonge whiche he ſpecyalli reherſyde the myracle that cryſte dyd in fedynge fyue thouſande people wythe fyue louys of brede and with iij lyttell fyſhys and thys frerys boy which caryd not gretely for hys maſter herynge hym ſay ſo and conſyderyng that his maſter was ſo great a churle and glotton anſwered with a loude voyce that all the church hard & ſayd by my trouth mayſter/ Then there were no fryers there. whiche anſwere made all the people to fall on ſuche a lawghynge that for ſhame the frere wente out of the pulpet. and as

---

[1] *v. M.*] Hazl. fyue M.   [2] *ij.*] Hazl. iii.
[3] *frerys*] in orig. fterys.

for the frerys boy he than departyd out of the church that the frere neuer saw hym after.

¶ By thys ye may se that it is honesty for a mā that is at mete to depart with suche as he has to them that be present.

xxxiv. *Of the frankelyne that wold haue had the frere gon.*

A[4] RYCHE fraynklyng dwellyng in the countrey[5] had a freer vsyng to his howse of whom he coud neuer be ryd & had taryed with him the space of a senyght & neuer depart[6] wherfore the fraynklyng beyng wery of hym/ on a tyme/ as he & his wyfe & this frere sat to geder at supper faynyd hym selfe very angry with hys wyfe In somoche he sayd he wolde bete her. This frere pseyuyng wel what they mēt sayd thus. master franklīg I haue bene here this seuenyght when ye were frēdys & I wyll tary here this fortenyght lenger but I wyll se you frendys agayne or I go.[7] thys man perseyuyng

---

[4] A wanting in orig.
[5] *in the countrey*] Hazl. countie.
[6] *& neuer depart*] Hazl. and wold never depart.
[7] *go*] Hazl. depart.

that he coude no good nor wolde not depart by
none honeſt meanys anſweryd hĩ ſhortly & ſayd
by god freere but thou ſhalte abyde here no lenger
& toke hym by the ſhulders & thruſt hym out of
the dorys by vyolence.¹

¶ By this ye may ſe that he that wyll lerne
no good by example/ nor good maner² to hym
ſhewyd is worthy to be taught with open re-
bukes.

xxxv. *Of the good man that ſayd to his wyfe he had yll³ fare.*

A parallel ſtory is found in the " Complete London
Jeſter," ed. 1771, p. 73.

FRER Lymytour⁴ come into a pore
mannys howſe in the countrey and be-
cauſe this pore man thought this frere
myght do hym ſome good he therfore thought to
make hym good chere/ But becawſe hys wyfe
wolde dreſſe hym no good mete for coſte/ he
therfor at dyner tyme ſayde thus/ By god wyfe

---

¹ *by vyolence*] Hazl. of the houſe.
² *nor good maner*] Hazl. in a maner.
³ *yll*] Hazl. euyll.
⁴ *Lymytour*] i. e. begging-friar.

bycawfe thou dyddeft dreffe me no good mete to my dyner/ were it nat for mafter frere/ thou fholdeft haue half a dofyn ftrypes. Nay fir quod the frere I pray you fpare nat for me/ wherwith the wyf was angry & therfore at foupper fhe caufed them to fare wors.

¶ By thys ye may fe it is good polycy for geftys yf they wyll haue any good chere to pleas alway the wyfe of the howfe.[5]

XXXVI. *Of the frere that bad hys chylde make a laten.*

Too imperfect to decipher in Hazl.
For an analogous account of the refults of inftruction in Latin, fee Bonaventure des Periers, " Les Contes ou les Nouvelles Récréations," &c. Nouv. Ed. par De la Monnaye, tom. i. Nouv. 23, Amfterd. 1735, p. 233 : " Du jeune fils qui fit valoir le beau Latin que fon Curé lui avoit monftré."

THERE was a frere whiche though he were well lernyd yet he was callyd wycked of condycyons whiche had a Gentylmannys fonne to wayte vpon hym and to teche hym to fpeke latyn.

[5] The moral is wanting in Hazl.

Thys frere came to thys chyldes fader dwellyng in he contrey/ and becawſe this frere wold haue this Gentylman to knowe that this chylde had metly well ſpent[1] his tyme for the whyle he had bene with hym/ he bad this chyld to make in latyn ſhortly Freres walke in the cloyſter. This chylde halfe aſtonyed bycawſe his maſter bad hym make this latyn ſo ſhortly anſwered at all aduentures and ſayd In circuitu impii ambulant.

xxxvii. *Of the gentylman that aſkyd the frere for his beuer.*

IN the terme tyme a good old gentylman beyng a lawyer cam to london to the terme & as he came he hapened to ouertake a frere which was ſom vnthryft & wet alone without his beuer wherfor this getylman aſked this frere where was his beuer that ſhold kepe hym copany and ſayd it was[2] contrary to his relygyon to go alone/ and it wolde cawſe people to ſuppoſe hym to be ſom apoſtata or ſome vnthryft. By god ſyr quod the frere my felow comendeth hym vnto your maſterſhyp/ why[3]

---

[1] *ſpent*] orig. reads ſpeut.   [2] *was*] in orig. waa.
[3] *why*] in orig. who.

quod the gentylman I knowe hym nat/ than quod the frere to the gentylman ye are the more to blame[4] to aſke for hym.

¶ By this tale ye may ſe that he that geueth coūſel to an vnthryft[5] and techeth hym his dutye ſhall haue oftentymes but a mocke for his labour.

XXXVIII. *Of the .iii.[6] men that chaſe the womā.*

The allotment of the two parts of a woman occurs in an old German poem, " Die Theilung." See Von der Hagen, " Geſammtabenteuer," vol. i. Stuttg. & Tübing. 1850, No. 18 :—

" 1475. Hêre wie habt ir iuch bedâht?
   iſt iuwer wille volbrâht,
   Welch teil ir nemen welt?"
   mit züchten antwurt' ir dir helt:
   " ſo wil ich, vrouw', an dirre ſtunt
1480 iu die rede tuon kunt,
   Und will es lenger niht verdagen,
   ich wil es ûf genâde ſagen : .
   Das oberſte teil ſol weſen mîn." &c.

Alſo in Don Juan Manuel, " El Conde Lucanor," No. 41, where the vice (el mal) leaves the upper half of a ſervant girl to the virtue (el bien) and keeps the lower part for

[4] *to blame*] Hazl. fole.
[5] *an vnthryft*] Hazl. any vnthryft.
[6] *iii.*] Hazl. thre.

herſelf. Imitated in one of G. E. Leſſing's poetical tales, "Die Theilung;" ſee Schriften, Berlin, 1838, vol. i. p. 210; alſo in "Lyrum Carum," 256.

THRE gentylmē cam into an Inne where a fayre woman was tapſter wherfor as theſe thre ſat ther makyng mery echone[1] of thē kyſſed her & made good paſtyme & pleſure. howbeit one ſpake meryly & ſayd I can not ſe how this gentylwoman is able to make paſtyme & pleaſure to vs all thre excepte that ſhe were departed in thre partes. By my trouthe quod one of theym/ yf that ſhe myght be ſo departed[2] than I wolde choſe for my parte her hed and her fayre face that I myght alway kyſſe her. Then quod the ſecōd I wold haue the breſt and hart for ther lyeth her loue. Then quod the thyrd then ther is nothyng left for me but the loynys buttokkys & leggys & I[3] am content to haue yt for my part. And when theſe gētylmen had paſſyd the tyme ther by the ſpace of one hour or ij they toke ther leue & were goynge away but or they[4] went the thyrd man that had choſen the bely & the buttokkys dyd kys the

[1] *echone*] Hazl. eche.
[2] *be ſo departed*] Hazl. be departed.
[3] *& I*] Hazl. I.
[4] *they*] orig. reads thye.

tapyſter & bad her farewel. what quod the furſt mã that had choſen the face & the mouth why doſt thou ſo/ thou doſt me wronge to kys my parte that I haue choſen of her. O quod the other I pray the be not angry for I wolbe⁵ cõtent that thou ſhalt kys my part for it.

xxxix. *Of the gẽtylmã that taught his cooke the medeſyne for the tothake.*

IN Eſſex there dwellyd a mery gentylman which had a cooke callyd Thomas that was gretly dyſeaſyd with the toth ake & complainyd to his mayſter there of whiche ſayd he had a boke of medycĩs & ſayd he wold loke vp his boke to ſe whether he cowd fynde any medecyn ther⁶ for it & ſo ſende one of hys doughters to his ſtudy for his boke and incontynent lokyd vppon yt a longe ſeaſon & than ſayde thus to hys coke. Thomas quod he here is a medeſyne for thy⁷ tothake & yt ys a charme but it wyll do you no good except ye knele on your knee⁸ and aſke yt for ſeynt charyte. Thys

---

⁵ *I wolbe*] Hazl. I am.
⁷ *thy*] Hazl. your.
⁶ *ther*] Hazl. therin.
⁸ *knee*] Hazl. knees.

man glad to be releaſyd of hys payne knelyd & ſayd mayſter for ſeīt charyte let me haue that medecyne. Then quod thys gentylman knele on your knees & ſay after me which knelyd doūe and ſayd after hym as he bad hym.

Thys gētylman began & ſayd thus. The ſone on the ſonday. The ſone on the ſonday quod thomas. The mone on the monday. The mone on the monday. the trynyte on the tewſday. the trinyte on the tewſday. The wite õ the wednyſ-day the wit on the wednyſday. The holy holy thurſday. The holy holy thurſday. And all that faſt on fryday. and al that faſt on fryday. Shite in thy mouthe on ſaterday. This Thomas coke herynge his mayſter thus mokkynge hym in an anger[1] ſtart vp & ſayd/ by goddys body mok-kyng churle I wyll neuer do the ſeruyce more. And wente forth to hys chāber to get hys gere to geder to thentent to gon thens by & by. But what for the anger that he toke with hys maſter for the moke that he gaue hym & what for labour that he toke to geder hys gere ſo ſhortly to geder the payne of the tothake wente from hym incontynent that his maſter com to hym & made hym tary ſtyll[2] & tolde hym that hys charme

---

[1] *in an anger*] Hazl. in anger.
[2] *tary ſtyll*] Hazl. to tarry ſtyll.

was the caufe of the eafe of the payn of his tothake.³

¶ By this tale ye may fe that anger oftymys puttyth away bodely payne.⁴

XL. *Of the gētylmā that promyſyd the ſcoler of Oxford a ſarcenet typet.*

Similar tales in Legrand d'Auſſy, fabliaux: "Les trois Aveugles de Compiègne," tom. iii. p. 1; Pellbartus, "Pomerium quadrageſimale," Aug. Vind. 1502, fol. i. ſermo 38 c. Benecke, "Beitraege zur Kenntniſs der altdeutſchen Sprache und Literatur, Bd. 2, Gottingen, 1832: "Der Pfaffe Amis," V. 2043-2472; Sozzini, Nov. 1; Franco Sacchetti, No. 140; Giov. Franc. Straparola, "XIII. Piacevoli Notti," No. 13, fav. 2. Alſo in "Nouveaux Contes à rire," Cologne, 1702: "Le Rotiſſeur Filouté," p. 261; and in "Scoggin's Jeſts," 1626: "How Scogin deceived the Draper," repr. 1864, p. 137.

SCOLER of Oxford lately made maſter of arte come to the cyte⁵ of lōdon & in polys met with the ſayd mery gētylmā of eſſex which was euer dyſpoſyd to playe many

³ *his tothake*] Hazl. the tothake.
⁴ *bodely payne*] Hazl. the bodely payne.
⁵ *come to the cyte*] Hazl. cam in to the cyte.

mery paieantys with whome before he had bene of famylier accoyntance and prayd hym to geue hym a fercenet typet. This gentylman more lyberall of promys than of gyft grantyd hym he fholde haue one yf he wolde come to his lodgynge to the figne of the bulle without byfhops gate in the next mornynge at vi of the cloke. Thys fcoler thanked hym & for that nyght departed to hys lodgynge in flete ftrete/ & in the mornynge erely as he poynted cam to hym to the fygne of the bull/ Anon as[1] this gentylman faw hym he bad hym go with hym in to the Cite & he fholde be fped anone/ which incontynent went togeder tyll they[2] cam in to feynt laurence churche[3] in the Jury wher the gentylman efpyed a preft rauefhyd to maffe & tolde the fcoler that yonder is the prefte that hathe the typet for you & bade hym knele down in the pewe & he wolde[4] fpeke to hym for it/ And incontynent this gentilman went to the preft and fayd Syr here is a fcoler and kynf-man of myne greatly dyfeafed with the chyn-cowgh.[5] I pray yow when maffe ys done gyue hym iij draughtys of your chales. The preft

---

[1] *Anon as*] Hazl. And as.
[2] *they*] in orig. fhe; Hazl. he.
[3] *churche*] in orig. churhe.
[4] *wolde*] Hazl. fhold.
[5] *chyncowgh*] i.e. hooping-cough.

graūted hym & turned hym to the ſcoler and
ſayd Syr I ſhall ſerue you as ſon as I haue ſayd
maſſe. the ſcoler thē taryed ſtyl & hard the maſſe
truſtīg then whan⁶ the maſſe was done that the
preſte wolde geue hym his typet of ſarcenet. Thys
gentylman in the meane whyle departed out of
the churche. This preſt whan maſſe was don
put wyne in the chalice & cam to the ſcoler
knelyng in the pew profferyng hym to drink of
the chales. this ſcoler lokyd vpon hym & muſed
& ſayd/ maſter perſon⁷ wherfore profer ye me
the chalyce mary quod the preſte for the gentylman tolde me ye were dyſeſyd with the chīcough
& prayd me therfore that for a medcyn ye myght
drynk of the chalis. Nay by ſeynt mary quod
the ſkolar he promyſyd me ye ſholdd delyūer me
a typet of ſercenet. Nay ſayde the preſte he ſpake
to me of no typet/ but he deſyryd me to gyue
you drynk of the chales for the chyncough. By
goddys body quod the ſcoler he is as he was euer
wont to be but a mockyng wrech/ & euer I lyue
I ſhall quyte it hym & ſo departyd out of the
churche ī gret āger.

¶ By thys tale ye may perceyue it were no
wyſdom for a man to truſt to a man to do a

---

⁶ *then whan*] Hazl. that whan.
⁷ *maſter perſon*] Hazl. why, maſter parſon.

thynge that ys contrary to hys olde accuſtumyd condycyons.

XLI. *Of maſter ſkelton that brought the byſhop of Norwich .ii. feſantys.*

The ſame ſtory, with very little alteration, in "Certain Merrie Tales of Skelton, Poet Laureat," 1567. See Skelton's Works, ed. A. Dyce, London, 1843, p. liii; compare "Scoggin's Jeſts:" "How Scogin was new chriſtened, and confirmed a Knave by the French biſhop," repr. 1864, p. 130.

IT fortuned ther was a gret varyaūce betwen the byſshop of Norwhich & one mayſter Skelton a poyet lauriat. In ſo moch that the byſshope cõmaunded hym that he ſholde nat come in at hys gatys.[1] This maſter ſkelton dyd abſent hym ſelfe for a longe ſeaſon but at the laſt he thought to do his duty to hym and ſtudyed wayes how he myght obtayn the byſhopys fauour and determynyd him ſelfe that he wold com to hĩ with ſome preſent & humble hym ſelfe to the byſhop & gat a couple of feſants and cam to the byſhoppys place & requyryd the porter he myght come in to ſpeke wyth my lorde.

[1] *in at hys gatys*] Hal. in his gatys.

this porter knowyng hys lordys pleafure wolde
not fuffer hym to come in at the gatys/ wherfore
this mafter fkelton went on the bak fyde to feke
fome other way to com in to the place. But
the place was motid that he cowd fe no waye to
come ouer except in one place where there lay a
longe tre ouer the motte in maner of a brydg that
was fallyn downe with wynd wherfore this mafter
fkelton went a long vppon the tre to com ouer &
when he was almoft ouer hys fote flyppid for
lake of fure fotyng & fell in to the motte vp to the
myddyl but at the laft he recoueryd hym felfe
& afwel as he coud dryed hym felfe agayn/ &
fodenly cam to the byfhop beyng in his hall then
lately ryfen from dyner which when he faw fkelton
cõmĩg fodĕly fayd to hym why thow chatyfe I
warnyd the thow fholdys neuer come yn at my
gatys & chargyd my porter to kepe the owt.

Forfoth my lorde quod fkelton though ye gaue
fuche charge & though your gatys be neuer fo
fuerly kept/ yet it is no more poffyble to kepe
me owt of your dorys than to kepe out crowes
or pyes for I cãe not in at your gatys. but I
came ouer the motte that I haue bene almoft
drownyd for my labour & fhewd hys clothys
how euyll he was arayed which caufyd many
that ftode thereby to laugh a pace. Then quod
fkelton yf it lyke your lordefhyp I haue brought

yow a dyſshe to your ſupper a cople of Feſantys.
Nay quod the byſhop I defy the and thy Feſantys
alſo And wreche as thou art pyke the out of my
howſe for I wyll none of thy gyft. How be it
with as humble wordys as he coud this ſkelton
deſyryd the byſhop to be hys good lorde & to
take his lytyll gyft of hym/ But the byſhop callyd
hym dawe[1] & fole often tymys & in no wyſe wolde
receyue that gyft. This Skelton than conſyderyng that the byſhop callyd hym fole ſo oft ſayd
to one of his famylyers therby that though it were
euyl to be criſtynyd a fole yet it was moche
worſe to be confyrmyd a fole of ſuche a byſhop
for the name of confyrmacyõ muſt nedes abyde/
therfore he ymagynyd how he might auoyd that
cõfyrmaciõ & muſyd a whyl & at the laſt ſayd to
the byſhop thus. if your lordſhyp knew the namys
of theſe feſãtys ye wold be cõtẽt to take them/
why caytyf quod the byſhop haſtely & angerly
what be theyre namys. I wys my lorde quod
ſkelton this Feſant is callyd alpha. ys. primus[2]
the furſt. & this is callyd O that ys nouiſſimus
the laſt. & for the more playn vnderſtandyng of
my mĩde. If it pleſe your lordſhyp to take them
I ꝑmyſe you This Alpha is the fyrſt that euer I
gaue you & this O is the laſt that euer I wyl

---

[1] *dawe*] i. e. fool.
[2] *ys. primus*] Hazl. which is in primys.

gyue you wyl I leue. at the which³ ãſwer al that wer by made gret laghter & al they deſyryd the byſhop to be good lord to hĩ for hys mery conceytys at whoſe⁴ requeſt or they went the byſhop was cõtent to take hym vnto his fauour⁵ agayn.

¶ By thys ye my ſe that mery conceytes dothe a man moche more good than to frete hym ſelfe with anger and melancoly.

XLII *Of the yeman of gard that ſayd he wold bete the carter.*

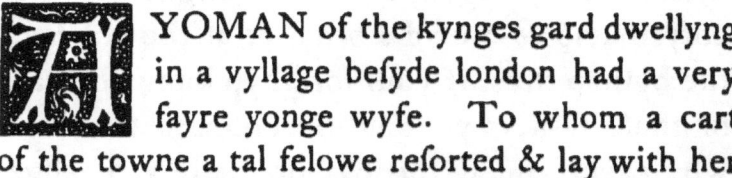

A YOMAN of the kynges gard dwellyng in a vyllage beſyde london had a very fayre yonge wyfe. To whom a cart of the towne a tal felowe reſorted & lay with her dyuers tymes whan her huſband was from home/⁶ & ſo⁷ openly knowẽ that all the town ſpake therof/ wherfor ther was a yong man of the towne well accoynted with this yemã of gard that tolde hym

---

³ *the which*] Hazl. which.
⁴ *whoſe*] Hazl. which.
⁵ *fauour*] orig. reads fauonr.
⁶ *was from home*] Hazl. was on garde.
⁷ *& ſo*] Hazl. and this was ſo.

that fuche a carter had layne by his wyfe. To whome thys yeman of garde fayd & fware by godys body that yf[1] he met hym[2] it fhold coft hym his lyfe. Mary quod the yong man yf ye go ftreyght euyn now the hye way ye fhall ouertak hym dryuīg of a cart[3] ladyn with hay toward london wherfore this yeman of garde[4] incontynent rode after this carter/ & within fhort fpace ouertoke hym & knew hym well ynough/ & incōtynent called the cart to hym & fayd thus. Sirra I vnderftand that thou doft ly euery night with my wyfe when I am from home. This carter beyng no thyng afrayd of the other/[5] anfwered ye mary what than/ what than quod the yeman of garde/ by goddes hart haddeft thou na tolde me the trouth[6] I wolde haue broken thy hede. And fo the yeman of garde retourned and no hurte done nor ftroke ftryken nor profered.

¶ By thys ye may fe that the greateft crakers fomtyme whan it cōmeth to the profe[7] be mofte cowardys.

[1] *that yf*] Hazl. if.
[2] *met hym*] Hazl. mette with hym.
[3] *of a cart*] Hazl. a cart.
[4] *of garde*] Hazl. of the garde.
[5] *of the other*] Hazl. of him.
[6] *trouth*] Hazl. truth.
[7] *profe*] orig. reads profe.

XLIII. *Of the pryſt that ſayd our lady was not ſo curyous a woman.*

IN the towne of Bottelley dwelled a mylner whiche had a good homely wench to his doughter whom a curat[8] of the next towne louyd/ and as the fame went had her at his pleſure.

But on a tyme this curat preched of theſe curyous wyues now a dayes/ & whether it were for the nones[9] or whether it come out at all aduenturys he hapned[10] to ſay thus in his ſermõ.

Ye wyues ye be ſo curious in all your warkes that ye wote nat what ye mene/ but ye ſhold folowe our lady. For our lady was nothynge ſo curyous as ye be/ but ſhe was a good homely wenche lyke the mylners doughter of bottellay. At which ſayng all the paryſhons made gret laughynge/ & ſpecyally they that knewe that he had loued[11] the ſame[12] wenche.

¶ By thys ye may ſe it is great foly for a man that is ſuſpected with any parſon to prayſe or

---

[8] *a curat*] Hazl. the curate.
[9] *for the nones*] i.e. for the purpoſe.
[10] *hapned*] Hazl. had penyd.
[11] *he had loued*] Hazl. he louyd.
[12] *the ſame*] Hazl. that ſame.

to name the fame parſon openly leſt it bryng hym forther in ſclaunder.

XLIV. *Of the fole that wold go to the deuyll.*[1]

This tale is taken from Joh. de Bromyard, "Summa Prædicantium," Litt. P, xii. § 39: "De quodam domino, qui fatuum ſuum infirmum frequenter cum per illum tranſiret, confortari ſolebat. dicendo: Spera in deo: ibis ad cœlum. Cui ille ſemper reſpondit: nolo illuc ire: a quo cum uno die quereret: quare nollet illuc ire. Reſpondit: quia volo ire ad infernum, quare inquit: quia inquit. diligo te: & ſicut fui tecum in vita, ita volo tecum eſſe in morte. & poſt mortem: & quia tu ibis ad infernum: ita volo ego ratione ſocietatis. Cui dominus. quomodo ſcis. quod ego illud vadam: quia inquit. tota patria loquitur ſic. dicentes. quod tu es peſſimus homo. et ideo ibis ad infernum: Et in veritate: qui malus homo fuit prius. ex verbis illius compunctus: optime ſe poſtea correxit." Repeated in Pauli, "Schimpff und Ernſt," Straſb. 1535, No. 43: "Von einem Narren der nit zu Gott faren wolt."

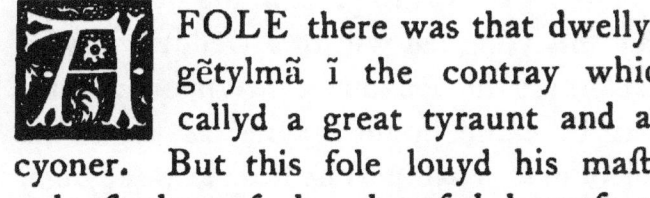

A FOLE there was that dwellyd with a gẽtylmã ĩ the contray whiche was callyd a great tyraunt and an ectorcyoner. But this fole louyd his maſter merueluouſly becauſe he cheryſyd hym ſo well. It

---

[1] Hazl. Of the fole that ſaide he had leuer go to hell than to heuen.

happenyd vppon a feafone one of the gentylmans
feruauntys fayde to the fole. as they talkyd of
fermon matters/ by my trowth Jak quod he
wolde to god that thou and I were both of vs
in heuyn. Nay by lady quod the fole I wyll
not go to heuyn for I had leuer go to hell/ than
the other afkyd hym why he had leuer go to
hell. By my trouth quod the fole for I wyll go
with my mafter & I am fure my mafter fhall go
to hell/ For euery man feyth he fhall go the
deuyll in hell therefore I wyll go thyther with
hym.

XLV. *Of the plowmannys fonne that fayd he faw
one make[2] a Gofe to kreke fweetly.*

THERE was a certayn ploughmannys
fonne of the contrey of the age ofe .xvi.
yeres that neuer come moche among
company but alwey wēt to plough and hufbandry/
on a tyme this yong lad wēt to a weddynge with
hys fader where he fee one lute vppon a lute.
And when he came home agayne[3] at nyght his
moder afkyd hym what fport he hade at weddynge.
This lad anfweryd and fayd by my trouth moder

[2] *make*] Hazl. to make.   [3] *home agayne*] Hazl. home.

quod he ther was one that brought in a gofe betwene hys armys[1] and tykled her fo vppõ the nek that fhe crekyd the fwetlyeft that euer I hard gofe creke in my lyfe.

XLVI. *Of the maydys anfwere that was with chylde.*

IN[2] a marchauntys houfe in london there was a mayd whiche was gotten[3] with chylde to whome the maftres of the houfe came & chargyd[4] her to tell her who was the fader of the chylde. To whome the mayden anfweryd forfoth no body/ why quod the mayftres yt ys not poffyble but fome mañe mufte be[5] the fader thereof. To whome the mayd fayd/[6] why maftres why may not I[7] haue a chylde without a man afwell as a hen to lay[8] eggys wythout a cok.

¶ Here ye may fe it is harde to fynde a woman wythout an excufe.

[1] *brought in a gofe betwene hys armys*] Hazl. brought a gofe in his armes.
[2] *In*] Hazl. At.   [3] *gotten*] Hazl. great.
[4] *& chargyd*] Hazl. and that commanded.
[5] *mufte be*] Hazl. is.   [6] *fayd*] Hazl. anfwered.
[7] *not I*] Hazl. I not.
[8] *a hen to lay*] Hazl. hennys lay.

XLVII. *Of the feruant that rymyd with hys mafter.*

In John Pet. de Memel, ed. 1695, No. 62, the fame ftory occurs; the German verfes are the more draftic, as the fervant's anfwer has no rhyme :—

>Ich heiffe Sylvefter
>Und fchlaf bei deiner Schwefter.

Der knecht antwortete :

>Junker ich heifs Hans,
>Und fchlaf bei Eurer Frau.

GENTYLMAN there was dwellynge nygh kyngfton vppon Temys. rydynge⁹ in the contrey wyth hys feruaunte which was not the moft quyckyft felow But rode alway fadly by hys mayfter and hade very few wordys. Hys mayfter fayde to hym Johñ quod he why rydyft fo fadly¹⁰ I wold haue the tell me fom mery talys to paffe¹¹ the tyme with. by my trouth mafter quod he I can tell no talys/ why quod the mafter¹² cãft¹³ not fyng. no by my trouth quod hys feruaunt¹⁴ I cõwd neuer fyng in

---

⁹ *rydynge*] Hazl. and rydynge.
¹⁰ *fo fadly*] Hazl. thou fo fadly.
¹¹ *paffe*] Hazl. beguyle.
¹² *why quod the mafter*] Hazl. Then fayd his mayfter.
¹³ *canft*] Hazl. canft thou.
¹⁴ *quod his feruaunt*] Hazl. quod he.

all my lyfe/ why quod the mafter¹ canft thou ryme than/² By my trouth mafter³ quod he I can not tell but yf ye wyll begynne to ryme I wyll folow as well as I can. by my trouthe quod the mafter that is well fayd⁴ than⁵ I wyll begyn to make a ryme let me fe howe well thou canft folowe/ fo the mafter mufyd a whyle⁶ and than began to ryme thus. Many mennys fwannes fwymmys in temmys and fo do myne.

Then quod the feruaunt. And manny men lye⁷ by other mennys wyues and fo do I by thyne/ what doft horfon⁸ quod the mafter/ by my trouth mafter nothynge quod he but make vp the ryme. but quod the mafter I charge the tell me why thou fayft fo/ forfothe mafter quod he for nothynge in the worlde but to make vp your ryme. Then quod the mafter yf thou do it⁹ for nothyng ellys

---

¹ *why quod the mafter*] Hazl. quod the mayfter.

² *ryme than*] Hazl. ryme.

³ *By my trouth mafter . . . I cannot tell*] Hazl. No by my trouthe . . . I can not.

⁴ *well fayd*] Hazl. well.

⁵ *fayd than*] Hazl. therfore.

⁶ *fo the mafter mufyd a whyle*] Hazl. thy mafter meanewhyle.

⁷ *And manny men lye*] Hazl. And many a man lyeth.

⁸ *horfon*] Hazl. thou, horefon.

⁹ *do it*] Hazl. doift.

I am content/[10] So the mafter forgaue hym his faynge all though he had fayd trewth.[11]

XLVIII. *Of the welchman that delyueryd the letter to the ape.*

The origin of this tale is again Joh. de Bromyard, " Summa prædicantium," Litt. J. viii. § 6: " Quidam aulam cuiusdam nobilis intrans : videnfque fymiam de fecta filiorum veftitum : quia dorfum ad eum habebat : filium credidit effe domini : cui cum reverentia qua debuit loqueretur : inuenit effe fymiam fuper eum chachinantem : cui ille malediceris inquit : credidi quod fuiffes iankyn filius domini mei." Reprinted in Th. Wright, " Latin Stories," &c. Lond. 1842, No. 129, " Filius domini." Imitated in " Jack of Dover," 1604; " The foole of Hampfhire;" " Percy Society," vol. iii. p. 30. It. in " Lyrum Carum," 141.

A KNYGHTE in Myddylfex had a feruaunt which had commytted a felony wherof he was endyted/ and becaufe the terme drew nye he fered he fholde be fhortly arayned therof & in ieoperdye of his lyfe. wherfor in all the hafte fent a letter by a walchmā a feruaunt of hys vnto the kynges Juftyce of the

---

[10] *content*] orig. reads concent.
[11] *he had fayd trewth*] Hazl. he fayd trouthe peraduenture.

kynges bench requyrynge hym to owe his lawfull fauour to hys feruant and cōmaunded hys feruant fhortly to brynge hym an anfwere/ This walche man came to the chefe Juftyce place and at the gate fawe an ape fyttynge there in a cote made for hym as they vfe to apparel apys for dyfport/ This walchman dyd of hys cap & made curtefy to the ape and fayd my mafter recōmendeth hym to my lorde your fader & fendeth hym here a letter. Thys ape toke thys letter and opened it and loked theron/ and after loked vpon the man makyng many mockes and mowes as the properte of apys is to do/ this welchman becawfe he vnderftode hym nat came agayn to his mafter accordyng to his cōmaundement and fayde he had delyuered the letter vnto my Lorde chefe Juftyces fonne whiche fat at the gate in a furred cote/ Anone his mafter afked hym what anfwere he had whiche fayd he gaue hym an anfwere but it was outher Frenche or Latyn for he vnderftode hym nat/ but fyr quod he ye nede nat to fear for I fawe by his countenance fo moche that I warant you he wyll do your errand furely[1] to my lorde hys fader. Thys gentylman in truft[2] therof made none other labour. For lacke wherof hys feruant that had done the felony

---

[1] *your errand furely*] Hazl. your errand.
[2] *truft*] orig. reads trnft.

within two dayes³ after was rayned at the kynges benche & caſt and afterwarde hangyd.

¶ By this ye may ſe that euery wyſe man ought to take hede that he ſende no folyſshe feruant vpon a haſty meſſage that is a mater of weyght.

XLIX. *Of hym that ſold ryght nought.*

Such difficult taſks or enigmatical queſtions are of very frequent occurrence in the literature of the middle ages. Generally known is the one taken from Juſtini, " Hiſtor. Philipp." lib. 18, cap. 3; repeated in " El libro de los enxemplos," No. 347; reprinted in " Bibl. de Aut. Eſpañ." tom. 51, Madr. 1860, and in Joh. Gallenſis, " Summa collectionum," pars ii. diſt. 1, cap. 4. s. l. 1493, fol. In another, firſt mentioned by Ratherius, (d. 974) " Sermo 3 de octavis paſchae," d'Achery, " Spicilegium," ed. 1723, fol. i. 395, (ſee Haupt, " Zeitſchrift f. deutſches Alterthum," vol. viii. p. 21), a man has to come to his prince half riding, half walking, and to bring with him his friend and his enemy; he comes with his right foot in the ſtirrup, walking with the left, and brings with him his dog as his beſt friend and his wife (whom he makes denounce him as a murderer) as his worſt enemy. This is repeated, with many alterations, in the " Geſta Romanorum," cap. 124; " Altdeutſche Blätter," ed. by Haupt and Hoffmann, Leipzig, 1836, vol. i. pp. 149, 154; " Scala celi," 50; Pauli, " Schimpff und Ernſt,"

---

³ *two dayes*] Hazl. a month.

1535, No. 400, fol. 75; Hans Sachs, Nürnberg, 1591, fol. vol. ii. p. 4, fol. 59, "Der Hecker mit den drei seltzamen stücken;" Die Schildbürger, cap. 21, in von der Hagen, Narrenbuch, Halle, 1811, p. 129; Ferd. Wolf, "Ueber die neuesten Leistungen der Franzosen für die Heraufgabe ihrer National-Heldengedichte," Wien, 1833, p. 135; Cf. Würdtwein, "Diocesis Moguntina in Archidiaconatus distincta," Mannhemii, 1749, tom. i. p. 488, and Loiseleur Deslongchamps, "Fables Indiennes," tom. ii. p. 125; "Cento Novelle Antiche," nov. 100, Torino, 1802, p. 183; and together with many similar jokes in "Salomon and Markolph" (in von der Hagen, Narrenbuch, p. 236, seq.) Finally, Grimm's "Kindermaerchen," Goettingen, 1856, No. 94 (cf. vol. iii. p. 170) contain a similar tale, "Die kluge Bauerntochter;" a girl has to come to the king not clothed, not naked; not riding, not driving; not in the way, not out of the way. She wraps a large fishing-net round her and comes dragged in the rut by a rope tied to the tail of an ass.

A CERTAYNE felow there was which proffered a dagger to sell to a felowe of his whiche answered hym and sayde that he had right nought to geue hym therfor. wherfor the other sayd that he shold haue his dagger vpon condycyon that he shoulde geue and delyuer vnto hym therfore within vi. dayes after right nought/ or els xl. shilynges in money/ wherto this other was content. Thys bargayn thus agreyd he that sholde delyuer thys ryght nought toke no thought vntyll suche tyme that the day apoynted drewe nye. At the whiche tyme he began[1] to Immagyne how he myght gyue hym[2] right nought. And fyrſt of all he thought on a feder/ a ſtrawe/ a pynnes poynte/ and ſuche other. But no thynge coud he deuyſe but that it was ſomwhat/ wherfor he come home al ſad & penſyfe for ſorow of leſynge of xl. ſhyllynges/ & coud nouther ſlepe nor take reſt/ wherof his wyfe beynge agreuyd demaūded the cawſe of his heuynes/ whiche at the laſt after many denayes tolde her all, well ſyr quod ſhe let me herewith alone & gete ye furthe a towne/ and I ſhall handle this[3] well ynough. This man folowynge his wyues councell went forthe of the towne & let his wyfe ſhyft.

This woman than henge vp an yerthen pot wherof the botom was out vpon the wall by a corde. And whan thys other man come and aſked for the good man ſhe ſayd that he was nat within/ But Syr quod ſhe I know your erand wel ynough/ For I wote well ye wold haue of myn huſbonde xl. ſhyllynges becauſe he can nat delyuer to you this day right nought/ Therfore ſyr quod ſhe put your hande into yonder potte and take your money/ this man beyng glad thruſt

[1] *he began*] in orig. be began.
[2] *hym*] Hazl. this man.
[3] *this*] Hazl. this matter.

his[1] hand in[2] fuppofyng to haue taken xl. fhyllynges of money & thruft his hand vp thrugh[3] vp to the elbow/ quod the wyfe than Syr what haue ye there. Mary quod he Ryght nought. Syr quod fhe than haue ye your bargeyn & than my hufbond hath contentyd you for his dagger accordynge to his promyfe.

¶ By this ye may fe that often tymes a womans wyt at an extremyte is moche better than a mannys.

L. *Of the frere that told the iii.[4] chylders fortunys.*

In Joh. Pet. de Memel, "Luftige Gefellfchaft," 1695, No. 253, p. 110, a friend gives the following reply to the queftion of a father about the employment his three fons fhould undertake: "If the one was a beggar, the other a thief and the third a murderer, they would all be well off for life," meaning thereby the fame profeffions the friar recommends in our tale. It. in Moncaut, "Contes populaires," 50; "Luftigmacher," 2, 50.

THERE was a certayn limytour which went a limytīge to a certeyn vyllage wherin dwelled a certayn ryche man of whome he neuer cowde gette the valew of an

---

[1] *his*] orig. reads hir. [2] *in*] Hazl. in it.
[3] *vp thrugh*] Hazl. thoroughe it. [4] *.iii.*] Hazl. thre.

halfpeny/ yet he thought he wolde go thyder agayn to aſſay[5] them. And as he went thyderward the wyfe ſtondynge at the dore perceyuynge him cõmynge a farre of thought that he wolde come thyder and by & by ran in & bad her chyldren ſtandyng at the dore that yf the frere aſked for her ſay ſhe was nat within. The frere ſaw her ron in and ſuſpected the cawſe and come to the dore and aſked for the wyfe/ the ſhyldren as they were byddyn/ ſayde that ſhe was not within/ than ſtode he ſtyl lokyng on the chyldren/ and at the laſt he called to hym the eldeſt & bad hym let hym ſe his hande/ and whan he had ſene his hande O Jheſu quod he what fortune for the is ordeyned/ Than called he the ſeconde ſonne to ſe his hande/ and his hande ſene the frere ſayde/ O lord what a deſteny is for the[6] preparyd. Than loked he in the thyrd ſoñes hand/ ſuerly quod he thy deſtenys is hardeſt of all/ & therwith wente he his way. The wyfe herynge theſe thynges ſodenly ran out and called the frere agayne/ and firſt made hym to come in/ and after to ſyt downe and ſet before hym the beſt mete that ſhe had/ and whan he had well etyn & dronken ſhe beſought hym to tell her the deſtenyes of her chyldren/ which at the laſt after

[5] *to aſſay*] Hazl. and aſſaye.
[6] *is for the*] Hazl. for the is.

many denayes tolde her that the fyrſt ſholde be a beggar. The ſecond a thefe. The third an homycyd/ whiche ſhe heryng fell downe in a ſowne & toke it greuouſly. The frere conforted her and ſayd/ that though theſe were theyr fortune yet there myghte be remedy had. Than ſhe beſought hym of his counſell. Than ſayd the frere ye muſt make the eldeſt that ſhalbe a begger a frere. and the ſecond that ſhalbe a thefe a man of law/ & the third that ſhalbe an homycyde/ a phiſycyon.

¶ By this[1] ye may lerne that they that wyll come to the ſpeche or Preſence of any parſon for theyr owne cawſe they muſt fyrſt endeuer theyme ſelfe to ſhewe ſuche maters as thoſe parſons moſte delyte in.

LI. *Of the boy that bare the frere hys maſters money.*

CERTAYN frere had a boy that euer was wont to bere this freres money and on a tyme whan the boy was farre behynde his maſter as they two walked togeder by the way there met a man the frere whiche knewe that the boy bare the frerys money and ſayde. How Mayſter frere/ ſhall I byd thy boy

---

[1] *this*] Hazl. this tale.

hye hym apace after the/ Ye quod the Frere Than went yᵉ man to yᵉ boy & fayd fyre thy mayfter byddyth yᵉ gyueth me xl. d.[2] I wyll not quod the boy then called the man with a hye voyce to yᵉ frere & fayd fyr he fayth he wyll not/ then quod the frere bete hym/ & when the boy herde his mayfter fay fo he gaue the man .xl. pens.

¶ By this ye may fe it is foly for a man to fay ye or nay to a matter except he knowe fuerly what the matter is.

LII. *Of Phylyp fpencer the bochers man.*

(Gerlach), "Eutrapeliarum," lib. ii. No. 58, p. 16, relates a very fimilar ftory; the butcher's name is David, and his fervant cries out to the friar, "You can have no more meat until you pay your bill." The fame in "Roger Bontems en belle Humeur," Cologne, 1731, tom. i. p. 119, "Naïveté d'un Valet:" "Point d'Argent point de Tripes;" and in "Nouveaux Contes à rire et Aventures plaifantes de ce Temps," 3ᵉ édit. Cologne, 1702, p. 102: "Sans Argent point de Tripes."

CERTAYN bocher dwellyng in faynt Nicholas flefhamels in london callyd Poule had a feruaũt callyd Peter. This Peter on a fonday was at yᵉ chirche heryng

[2] .*xl. d.*] Hazl. xl pens.

maſſe & one of his felawes whoſe name was Phylip ſpencer was ſent to call hym at the comaundement of his mayſter. So it happened at the tyme that the curat prechyd. And in his ſermon touched many auctorytees of the holy ſcrypture. Amonge all the wordes of the pyſtell of ſaynt Poule ad philippenſes/ that we be[1] not onely bound to beleue in cryſt but alſo to ſuffer for cryſtys ſake & ſayd theſe wordes in ye pulpet/ what ſayth Poule ad philippenſes to this. This yõge man y^t was called Philip ſpencher had went he had ſpoken of hym anſwered ſhortely & ſayd/ mary ſyr he bad Peter come home & take his parte of a podyng for he ſholde go for a calfe anone. The curat heryng this was abaſhyd & all the audyence made grete laughter.

¶ By this tale[2] ye may lerne[3] that it is no token of a wyſe man to gyue a ſodayne anſwere to a queſtiõ before that[4] he knowe ſuerly what the matter is.

[1] *that we be*] Hazl. howe be.
[2] *this tale*] Hazl. this.
[3] *lerne*] Hazl. ſe.
[4] *before that*] Hazl. before.

LIII. *Of the courtear and the carter.*

A corresponding tale in "Scoggin's Jests;" "How Scogin told those that mocked him, that hee had a wall-eye." Reprint. 1864, p. 106.

THER came a courtyer by a carter the whiche in derysyon preysed the carters bak legges and other members of his body merueloufly whofe geftyng the carter perceyued & fayd he had another property than ye courtyer efpyed in hym/ & whan the courtyer had demaūded what it fholde be/ he loked afyde ouer his fholder vpon the courtyer & fayd thus/ lo fyr this is my properte.

I haue a wall eye in my hed/ for I neuer loke ouer my fholder this wyfe but I lyghtly efpye a knaue.

¶ By this tale a man maye fe that he that vfed to deryde and mocke other folkys/ is fomtyme hym felfe more deryded & mocked.

LIV. *Of the yonge man that prayd his felow to tech hym his pater nofter.*

In the "Nouveaux Contes à rire," &c. Cologne, 1702, p. 248, "D'un Homme à qui on apprit à prier à Dieu," a corresponding tale occurs; the prieſt uſes a very effective means of teaching the Pater noſter to a niggard pawnbroker: he bids him lend money to all the people he ſhould ſend him. So he firſt ſends a man called "Pater noſter," living at a place called "Qui es in cœlis," then another of the name of "Sanctificetur," coming from "Nomen tuum," &c.

YONG mã of yᵉ age of .xx. yere rude & vnlernyd in yᵉ tyme of lẽt cã to his curat to be cõfeſſyd¹ whiche whẽ he was of his lyfe ſerched & examyned coude not ſay his Pater noſter/ wherfore his cõfeſſour exorted hym to lerne his Pater noſter/ & ſhewed hym what an holy & goodly prayer it was/ & the effect therof/ & the vii petycyons therin cõteyned. The fyrſt petycyõ begynneth. Pater noſter. &c. yᵗ is to ſaye. O fader halowyd be thy name amõge mẽ in erth as amõge aũgels in heuen. The ii. Adueniat. &c. Let thy kyngdome come & regne thou amonge vs men in erth as amonge aũgels in heuen. The .iii. Fiat. &c. Make vs to fulfyl thy wyll here in erth as thy aũgels in heuen. The .iiii. Panẽ noſtrũ. &c. Gyue vs our dayly ſuſtenaũce alwaye & helpe vs as we gyue & helpe² them yᵗ haue nede of vs. The .v. Dimitte. &c. Forgyue vs our ſynnes

---

¹ *confeſſyd*] orig. reads toſeſſyd.
² *gyue & helpe*] Hazl. haue and helpe.

done to the as we forgyue them yᵗ trefpas agaynfte vs. The .vi. Et ne nos. Let vs not be ouercome with euyll temptacyõ. The .vii. Sed libera. &c. But delyuer vs frõ all euyll amen.

And then his confeffour after this expofycyõ to hym made inioyned hym in penaũce to faft euery fryday brede & water³ tyll he had his Pater nofter well & fuffycyẽtly lerned. This yonge man mekely acceptyng his penaunce fo departed & came home to one of his cõpanyons & fayd to his felow. fo it is that my goftly fader hath gyuen me in penaũce to faft euery fryday brede & water tyll I can fay my Pater nofter/ therfore I pray yᵉ teche me my Pater nofter/ & by my trouth I fhall therfore teche the a fonge of Robyn hode that fhall be worth .xx. of it.

¶ By this tale ye maye lerne to knowe the effect of the holy prayer of the Pater nofter.

LV. *Of the frere that prechyd in ryme expownyng the aue maria.*

The latter portion of this tale is repeated in "Scoggin's Jefts," 1626, Mr. Hazlitt's reprint, p. 76.

³ *brede & water*] Hazl. on brede and water.

CERTAYN frere there was whiche upō our lady day the Annūcyacyon made a fermon in the whyte frerys in London/ and began his anteteme¹ this wyfe/ Aue maria gracia plena dominus tecū/ &c.

Thefe wordes quod the frere were fpoken by the aungel Gabryel to our lady when fhe cōceyued Cryft/ whiche is as moche to fay in our moder tōgue as all heyle Mary well thou be ye fone of god is w^t the. And further more the aūgell fayd/ thou fhalte conceyue and bere a fone. And thou fhalt call his name Jefum/ and Elyzabeth thy fwete cofyn/· fhe fhall conceyue the fwete faynt Johñ. And fo procedyd ftyll in his Sermon in fuche fond ryme that dyuers & many gentylmen of the court that were there begā to fmyle & laugh. The frere y^t perceyuynge fayd thus Mayfters I pray you harke I fhall tel you a narraciō.

There was ones a yong preeft y^t was not all the beft clark fayd maffe & rede a colect thus Deus qui viginti filij tui &c. Where² he fholde haue fayd vnigeniti filij tui. &c.

And after whē mas was done there was fuche a gentylmā as one of you are³ now y^t had herde

---

¹ *anteteme*] Hazl. antetexte.   ² *Where*] Hazl. wherfore.
³ *are*] orig. reads at.

his maſſe came to yᵉ preeſt & ſayd thus. Syr I pray you tell me how many ſonnys had god almyghty/ quod yᵉ preeſt why aſke you yᵗ. Mary ſyr quod yᵉ gentylman I ſuppoſe he had .xx. ſonnys/ for ye ſayd ryght now. Deus qui viginti filii tui. The preeſt perceyuyng how yᵗ he derydyd hym anſwerde hym ſhortly & ſayd thus. How many ſonnys ſo euer god almyghty had/ I am ſure yᵗ thou art none of them for thou ſkornyſt yᵉ worde of god. And ſoo ſayd the frere in the pulpet. No more ar ye none of yᵉ chylderē of god. For ye ſkorne & laugh/ at me now yᵗ preche to you the worde of god. which wordys made the gentylmen and all the other people laughe moche more thā they dyd before.

¶ By this tale a man may lerne to perceyue well yᵗ the beſt the wyſyſt & yᵉ moſt holyeſt matter yᵗ is by found pronunciatyon & vtteraūce may be marryd/ nor ſhall not[4] edyfye to yᵉ audyēce. Therfore euery proces wolde be vtteryd with wordys & cōtenaūce cōuenyent to the matter.

Alſo yet by this tale they that be vnlernyd in yᵉ latyn tongue maye knowe the ſentence[5] of the aue maria.

[4] *nor ſhall not*] orig. reads nor ſhall nor.
[5] *ſentence*] Hazl. ſeſtence.

LVI. *Of the curat that prechyd the artycles of the Crede.*

The " Miracle-play" alluded to in this story is not contained in the collection of pageants known under the name of " Ludus Coventriæ," (published by the Shakespeare Society: " Ludus Coventriæ; a Collection of Mysteries," edited by J. O. Halliwell, London, 1841), and represented at Coventry on the Feast of Corpus Christi, as the twelve Articles of the Creed are not mentioned in any of them. According to Collier, " The History of the English Dramatic Poetry," vol. ii. Lond. 1831, p. 138, the MS. preserved in the British Museum (" Bibl. Cotton. Vespas." D. viii.) was written at least as early as the reign of Henry VII, and therefore it may well be that at the time the " Hundred Mery Talys" were compiled, or, at any rate, the present tale was written, another series of " Mysteries" was performed at Coventry on that occasion. This supposition is confirmed by a notice from the " MS. Annals, Codex Hales," quoted by Th. Sharp in his " Dissertation on the Pageants or Dramatic Mysteries anciently performed at Coventry," Coventry, 1825, 4to. p. 11: " 1519-20. New Plays at Corpus Christi Tyde which were greatly commended."

There is, however, another collection of " Mysteries," the " Chester Plays, formerly represented by the trades of Chester at Whitsuntide," (edited as one of the publications of the Shakespeare Society, by Th. Wright, vol. i. Lond. 1843; vol. ii. Lond. 1847,) which has in the play No. 22, " The Emission of the Holy Ghost," (vol. ii. p. 134,) the very verses alluded to in the present tale. As this work is not in everybody's hands I think myself justified in quoting the verses in full:

"*Petrus.*

I beleeve in God omnipotente,
That made heaven and eirth and firmament,
With fteadfafte harte and trewe intente,
And he is my comforte.

Andreas.

And I beleeve more I be lente,
In Jefu his fonne from heavenfente,
Vereye Chrifte that us hath kente,
And is our elders lore.

Jacobus Major.

And I beleeve, with bofte,
In Jefu Chrifte, in mighteft mofte,
Confeveith through the holye ghofte,
And borne was of Marye.

Johannes.

And I beleeve, as I cane fee,
That under Pilate fuffred he,
Skourged and nayled on roode tree,
And buryed was his fayer bodye.

Thomas.

And I beleeve, and fouth can tell,
That he ghoftlye wente to helle:
Delivered his that their did dwell,
And rofe the thirde daie.

Jacobus Minor.

And I beleeve fully this,
That he fteyed up to heaven bleffe,
And on his fathers righte hande is,
To raigne for ever and aye.

Philippus.

And I beleeve, with harte fteadfafte,
That he will come at the lafte,
And deeme mankinde as he has cafte,
Bouth the quicke and the dead.

Barthelemewe.

And my beleffe fhalbe mofte
In vertue of the holye ghofte,
And through his helpe, without bofte,
My life I thinke to leade.

Mathieus.

And I beleeve, through Godes grace,
Suche beleffe as holye chourch has,
That Godes bodye graunted us was
To ufe in forme of bredde.

Symon.

And I beleve with devocion
Of fynne to have remiffion,
Through Chriftes bloode and paffion,
And heaven, when I am dead.

Jude.

And I beleeve, as all we mon,
In the generall refurrexcion
Of eiche bodye, when Chrifte is borne
To deme bouth good and evill.

Matheus.

And I beleeve, as all we maye,
Everlaftinge life after my daye
In heaven to have ever and aye,
And fo overcome the devill."

In a third collection, the "Towneley Myſteries," which might poſſibly have contained correſponding verſes, "The Emiſſion of the Holy Ghoſt" is loſt by a lacuna in the MS.

IN a vyllage in warwyck ſhere there was a paryſhe preeſt & thoughe he were no gret clark nor graduat of yͤ vnyuerſyte/ yet he prechyd to his paryſhons vpõ a ſonday/ declaryng to thẽ yͤ .xii. artycles[1] of the Crede. ſhewynge them that the fyrſt artycle was to beleue in god the fader almyghty maker of heuen & erth. The ſecond. To beleue in Jeſu Cryſte his onely ſone our lorde coequall with yͤ fader in all thynges perteynyng to yͤ deyte. The thyrd that he was cõceyuyd of the holy gooſt Borne of the vyrgyn Mary. The fourth that he ſuffred deth vnder ponce pylate/ & that he was crucyfyed dede & beryed. The fyft that he deſcendyd to hel & fet[2] out yͤ good ſowlys yͭ were in fayth & hope/ & that he[3] yͤ thyrd day roſe from deth to lyfe. The ſyxth he aſſendyd in to heuen to yͤ ryht ſyde of god yͤ fader wher he ſyttyth. The ſeuenth yͭ he ſhall come at the day of dome to Judge both vs that be qvik &

---

[1] *the .xii. artycles*] Hazl. xii. artycles.
[2] *fet*] i. e. fetched.
[3] *and that he*] Hazl. and than.

them that be dede. The eyght to beleue in the holy gooſt equall god w^t the fader & the ſone. The nynth in holy chyrche[1] Catholyke & in the holy comunyõ of ſayntys. The tenth In ye remyſſyon of ſynnes. The leuynth In the reſurreccyõ generall of ye body and ſoule. The twelfth In euerlaſtynge lyfe that god ſhall rewarde thẽ that be good. And ſayd to his paryſhons further y^t theſe artycles ye be bounde to beleue for they be trew &[2] of auctoryte. And yf you beleue not me/ thẽ for a more ſuerte & ſuffycyẽt auctoryte/ go your way to couentre/ and there ye ſhall[3] ſe them all playd in corpus criſti playe.

¶ By redyng of this tale they y^t vnderſtõde no latyn may lerne to knowe the .xii. articles of the fayth.

LVII. *Of the frere that prechyd the .x. comaundementys.*

The diviſion of the Decalogue followed in this tale is taken from Exodus xx; it was adopted by the Council of Trent and uſed by the whole Latin Church. Luther approved of it, and it is ſtill in uſe with the entire Lutheran denomination. The diviſion now employed by the Church of England is the ſame which has always been uſed by the

---

[1] *holy chyrche*] Hazl. the holy churche.
[2] *trew &*] Hazl. trewe.
[3] *ſhall*] orig. reads ye ye ſhall.

Greek Church. It was ſtrongly recommended by Calvin in 1536, adopted by Bucer and the Tetrapolitans, and is to be found in any Engliſh formulary ſince 1537. Mr. Hazlitt's conjecture for the lacuna in his edition, p. 82, is therefore inadmiſſible; and this is more clearly ſhown by the fact, that in his interpolation either the ſeventh or eighth commandment is omitted. To judge from the undamaged paſſages, however, there muſt have been ſome difference between Mr. Hazlitt's original and mine: the text of the mutilated copy cannot have read but thus: *The eighth, not to bear falſe witneſs againſt thy neighbour.* THE NINTH AND TENTH, *not to couete nor deſyre no mannes goodes vnleſully. Thou ſhalt not deſyre thy neyghbours wyfe,* &c., this being exactly the form, which was nearly excluſively uſed ſince its acceptation by the Council of Trent Catechiſm. It is likewiſe found in Maſkell's and Biſhop Hilſey's Primers.

The ſeven deadly ſins have always been the ſame, but their diviſion is ſometimes different. See Mr. Hazlitt's edition, p. 83, note 2, and Maſkell's "Prymer," in "Monum. . Ritual. Eccles. Anglic." vol. ii. p. 178, London, 1846.

 LIMITOUR of the gray frerys in London whiche prechyd in a certayn vyllage in the countrey in the tyme of his lymitacyõ/ & had but one ſermõ⁴ which he had lerned by hart yᵗ was⁵ of yᵉ declaryng of the .x. cõmaũdemẽtes. The fyrſt to beleue in one god/ & to honour hym aboue all thynge. The

---

⁴ *& had but one ſermon*] Hazl. and had prechyd a ſermon.   ⁵ *that was*] Hazl. that.

secõd to swere not in vayn by hym nor none other¹ of his creatures. The thyrde to abstayne from worldly operacyõ on yᵉ holy day thou & all thy seruantys of whõ thou hast charge. The fourthe to honor thy parẽtys & helpe thẽ in theyr necessyte. The fyfth to sle no man in dede nor wyll nor for no hatred² hurte his body nor good name. The syxt to do no fornycacyõ actuall/ nor by no vnlefull thought to desyre no fleshly delectacyõ. The seuenth to stele nor depryue no mãnes goodes by thefte robbery extorcyõ/ vsery/ nor dysceyt. The eyght to bere no false wytnesse to hurt another/ nor to tell no lyes/ nor to say nothyng agaynst trewthe. The nynth to couet nor desyre no mañys goodes vnlefull. The tenth to couet nor to desyre³ thy neyghbours wyfe for thyn owne appetyte vnlefully.

And because this frere had preched this sermon so oftyn/ one yᵗ had hard it before told the frerys seruaũt yᵗ his mayster was callyd frere Johñ .x. cõmaũdementes wherfor this seruaũt shewed yᵉ frere his mayster therof/ and aduysed hym to preche some sermon of some other matter/ for it greuyd hym to here his mayster so deryded/ & to

---

¹ *none other*] Hazl. none.
² *hatred*] Hazl. orig. reads hated.
³ *The tenth to couet nor to desyre*] Hazl. thou shalt not desyre.

be called frere Johñ .x. cõmaũdemẽtys/ for euery man knoweth what ye wyll say as soone as euer ye begyn bycause ye haue preched it so oft.

Why than quod y͏ͤ frere I am sure thou knowest well which be y͏ͤ .x. cõmaũdementys y͏ͭ hast harde thẽ so oft declaryd/ ye syr quod the seruaũt y͏ͭ I do. Then quod the frere I praye the reherse thẽ vnto me now. Mary quod y͏ͤ seruaũt these be they.[4] Pryde Couetyse Slouth Enuy wrath Glotony and Lechery.

¶ By redynge this tale ye maye lerne to knowe the .x. cõmaundementes and the .vii. dedely synnes.

LVIII. *Of the wyfe that bad her husband ete the candell furst.*

This tale is imitated by John Cotgrave, "Wits Interpreter, the English Parnassus," 1662, p. 282.

HE husbande sayde to his wyfe thus/ wyfe[5] by this candell I dremed this nyght that I was a cokolde.[6] To whome she answered and sayd husbonde. By

---

[4] *these be they*] Hazl. they be these.
[5] *to hys wyfe thus/ wyfe*, &c.] Hazl. to his wyfe thus wyfe, &c.
[6] *a cokolde*] Hazl. cocke colde.

this brede ye are none. Thē fayd he/ wyfe ete the brede. She anfwerd & fayd to her hufbande/ then ete you the candell for you fware fyrft.

¶ By this a man may fe that a womans anfwere is neuer to feke.

LIX. *Of the man of lawys fonnys anfwer.*

WOMAN demaūdyd a queftyon of a yong[1] chyld fonne vnto a mā of lawe of what craft his fader was/ which chyld fayd his fader was a crafty man of lawe.

¶ By this tale a man may perceyue that fometyme peraduenture yōge Innocentys fpeke truely vnduyfed.

LX. *Of the frere in the pulpit that bad the woman leue her bakelyng.*

IN a certayn paryfh chyrche in London after the olde lawdable & accuftomyd maner there was a frere mynor all though he were not the beft clark nor coude not

[1] *yong*] Hazl. little.

make the beſt ſermon/ yet by the lycence of the curat he there preched to the paryſhons.² Among the whiche audyence there was a wyfe at that tyme lytyll dyſpoſyd to contemplacyõ talkyd with a goſyp of hers of other feminyne tales/ ſo loud that the frere hard & ſomwhat was perturbyd therwith. To whom therfore openly the frere ſpake & ſayd. Thou woman there in the tawny gow/³ hold thy peace & leue thy babelyng thou troblyſt the worde of god.

This woman there with ſodeynly abaſhyd bycauſe ye frere ſpake to her ſo openly y^t al ye people her beheld anſweryd ſhortly & ſayd/ I beſhrewe hye hard⁴ that babelyd more of vs two. At ye whyche ſeyng ye people dyd laugh bycauſe they felt but lytyll fruyte in his ſermon.

¶ By this tale a man may lerne to be ware how he openly rebukyth any other & in what audyence leſt it tourne⁵ to his owne reproſe.

> ² *paryſhons*] orig. reads paryſhous.
> ³ *gow*] Hazl. gowne.
> ⁴ *hye hard*] Hazl. his harte.
> ⁵ *tourne*] Hazl. come.

LXI. *Of the welchman that caſt the ſkot in to the ſee.*

IN the rayne of the moſt myghty and vyctoryous Prynce kynge Henry the .viii. cruell warre began betwene Englyſshe men Frenſhemen/ & Skottys. The Englyſshemen were ſo myghty vpon yᵉ ſe that none other people of other realmys were able to reſyſt thẽ/ wherfore they toke many grete enterpryſys/ & many ſhyppys/ & many pryſoners of other remys yᵗ were theyr enmys. Among the which they happenyd on a ſeaſon to take a ſkottys ſhyp. & dyuers ſkottys they ſlew & toke pryſoners. Among whom ther was a welchmã that had one of the ſkottys pryſoner & bad hym that he ſhold do of his harnes/ which to do the Skot was very loth/ howbeyt for fere at yᵉ laſt he pullyd it of wᵗ an yuyll wyll/ & ſayde to yᵉ welchmã/ yf thou wilt nedys haue my harnes take it there/ & caſt it ouer the bord in to the ſe. The welchman ſeyng that ſayd. By Cottes blut & her nayll. I ſhall make her fat¹ it agayn. And toke hym by yᵉ legges & caſt hym after ouer the bord in to the ſe.

¶ By this tale a man maye lerne yᵗ he that is

---

¹ *fat*] i.e. fetch.

fubget to another ought to forfake his owne wyll/ & folow his wyll & cõmaũdement yᵗ fo hath fubieccyon ouer hym/ left it torne to his gretter² hurt & damage.

LXII. *Of the man that had³ the dome wyfe.*

The fame ftory in the "Scolehoufe of Women," 1542. Reprinted in (Utterfon's) "Select Pieces of Early Popular Poetry," vol. ii. p. 73-74, Lond. 1825.

HERE was a man that maryed a woman whiche hath grete ryches & bewte/ how be it fhe had fuche an impedyment of nature that fhe was dome and coude not fpeke/ whiche thynge made hym full ofte to be⁴ ryght pẽfyfye & fad/ wherfore vpon a daye as he walkyd alone ryght heuy in hart thynkĩg vpõ his wyfe. Ther came one to hym & afkyd hym what was the caufe of his heuynes/ which anfweryd that it⁵ was onely bycaufe his wyfe was borne dome. To whõ this other fayd. I fhall fhewe yᵉ foone a remedy & a medycyn therfore that is thus. Go take an afpen lefe & lay it vnder her tõgue this nyght fhe beyng a flepe/ & I warrant the yᵗ

---

² *gretter*] Hazl. great. ³ *had*] orig. reads bad.
⁴ *full ofte to be*] Hazl. to be. ⁵ *it*] in orig. is.

ſhe ſhall ſpeke on the morow/ whiche man beyng glad of this medycyne preparyd therfore/ & gatheryd aſpen leues. Wherfore he layd .iii.[1] of them vnder her tõge whẽ ſhe was a ſlepe. And vpon yᵉ morowe whẽ he hym ſelf wakyd he deſyrous to know how his medycyne wroughte beyng in bed wᵗ her demaunded[2] of her how ſhe dyd/ & ſodenly ſhe anſweryd & ſayd. I beſhrewe your hart for wakynge me ſo erly/ & ſo by vertew of yᵗ medycyne ſhe was reſtored to her ſpeche.

But in cõcluſyon her ſpeche ſo increſyd day by day & ſhe was ſo curſt of cõdycyõ that euery day ſhe braulyd & chyde[3] with her huſbande ſo moche yᵗ at yᵉ laſt he was more vexyd and had moche more troble & dyſſeaſe with her ſhrewed wordes then he had before whan ſhe was dome.

Wherfore as he walked another tyme alone he happened to mete agayne with the ſame perſon that taught hym the ſayde medycyne. And ſayde to hym this wyſe.

Syr ye taught me a medycyne but late to make my dome wyfe to ſpeke. Byddyng me laye an aſpen lefe vnder her tonge when ſhe ſlepte. And I layd .iii. aſpen leues there. wherfor now ſhe

---

[1] *.iii.*] Hazl. thre.
[2] *demaunded*] Hazl. he demaunded.
[3] *chyde*] i. e. made an inceſſant noiſe.
[4] *alone*] Hazl. abrode.

speketh. But yet she speketh so moche and so shrewdly that I am more wery of her now than I was before when she was dome.

Wherfore I praye you teche me a medycyne to modyfye her that she speke not so moche.

This other answeryd and sayd thus. Syr I am a deuyll of hell. But I am one of them that haue leest power there. Albeyt yet I haue power to make a woman to speke. But yet yf[5] a woman begyn ones to speke/ I nor all the dyuels in helle that haue the most[6] power be not able to make a woman to be styll/ nor to cause her to leue her spekynge.

¶ By this tale ye may note that a man oftymes desyreth and coueteth to moche[7] that thynge that oft torneth to his dysplesure.

LXIII. *Of the proctor of arches that had the lytell wyfe.*

This tale may be taken from Ottomarus Luscinius, "Joci ac Sales mire Festivi," s. l. 1524, 8vo. No. 50, sign. D 3, *verso*: "Mulier parva minus malum," where it is told of Aristoteles; it was appropriated by Joh. Gastius, "Convivalium Sermonum," lib. i. p. 313, Basil, 1549:

[5] *But yet yf*] Hazl. but and if.
[6] *the most*] Hazl. the more.
[7] *to moche*] Hazl. moche.

"De uxore parva," and alſo by E. Walgemuth, " 500 Friſche und verguldete Haupt-Pillen," s. l. 1669, ii. No. 30, p. 56. In the "Nouveaux Contes à rire," &c. Cologne, 1702, it is told of Leonidas of Lacedemon, and is likewiſe contained in the "Complete London Jeſtes," 1771, p. 65; Certayne Conceyts, 14; Conceits, 81; repr. in Shakeſp. "Jeſt Books," iii. pp. 8, 24. Item, Lyrum Carum, 87; Schreger, 17, 114, p. 567.

NE aſkyd a proctoure of Arches lately before maryed why he chaſe hym ſo lytell a wyfe/ whiche anſwerede becauſe he had a text ſaynge thus. Ex duobus malis minus malum[1] eſt eliendum/ that is to ſaye in englyſshe. Amonge euyll thynges the leſt is to be choſen.

LXIV. *Of the .ii.[2] nonnys that were ſhryuyn of one preſt.*

IN the tyme of lente there cam two nonnys to ſaynt Johns in london by- cauſe of the greate pardon there to be confeſſyd. Of yᵉ whiche nonnys the one was a yonge lady & the other was olde. This yonge lady choſe fyrſt her Confeſſoure/ and confeſſyd her that ſhe had ſynned in Lechery. The con-

[1] *minus malum*] Hazl. minus malis.
[2] *the .ii.*] Hazl. ii.

feſſoure aſked w*t* whom it was. She ſayde it was with a luſty Gallãt. He demaũdyd where it was. She ſayd in a pleaſaunt grene herber. He aſkyd further whẽ it was. She ſayd in y*e* mery moneth of May. Then ſayd y*e* confeſſour this wyfe. A fayre yong lady/ with a luſty gallant/ in a pleaſaunt herber/ in y*e* mery³ moneth of May/ ye dyd but your kynde. Now by my trouth god forgyue you & I do.

And ſo ſhe departed and incõtynent the olde nõne met with her aſkynge her how ſhe lyked her confeſſour/ whiche ſayde that he was⁴ the beſt goſtly fader y*t* euer ſhe hadde And the moſt eaſyſt in penaunce geuynge.

For cõfort wherof this other nonne went to the ſame confeſſour. And ſhroue her lykewyſe that ſhe had ſynned in Lechery. And he demaunded with whom/ which ſayde with an olde Frere/ he aſkyd where. She ſayd in her olde cloyſter. He aſkyd what ſeaſon. She ſayd in lent. Then the confeſſour ſayd thus.

An olde hore to lye with an olde frere/ in the olde cloyſter/ in the holy tyme⁵ of Lent. By cokkys body yf god forgyue the yet wyll I neuer forgyue the.

³ *in the mery*] Hazl. and in the mery.
⁴ *that he was*] Hazl. he was.
⁵ *in the holy tyme*] Hazl. and in the holy tyme.

Whiche wordys caufyd her to departe all fad and fore abasfhyd.

¶ By this tale men may lerne that a vycyoufe acte is more abhomynable in one perfon than in an other/ in one feafon than in an other and in one place than in an other.

LXV. *Of the efquyer that fholde haue bene made knyght.*

WHEN the moft noble and fortunate prynce Edwarde of Englonde made warre in Fraunce with greatte puyffaunce and Armye of People. Whome the Frenche kynge with a nother grete hoft incounteryd. And when bothe ye hoftis fhulde Joyne & the trumpettis began to blow/ a yong fquyer of englonde rydyng on a lufty courfer of whiche horfe the noyfe of ye trūpettys fo prykkyd ye courage y^t the fquyer coude not hym retayne/ fo that agaynft his wyll he ran vpon his enemys whiche fquyer feynge none other remedy fet his fpere in the reft/ and rode trough the thykkyft of his enemys/ & in conclufyon had good fortune and fauyd hymfelfe alyue without hurt/ & the englyfh hoft folowyd & had the vyctory. And after when ye felde was done¹ this kyng Edwarde called the fquyer/ & bad hym knele downe for he wolde make hym knyght/ becaufe y^t² he valyauntly was ye man³ y^t day which with the moft couragyoufe ftomak aduenturyd fyrft vpon theyr enemys. To whom ye fquyre thus anfwerde. Yf it lyke your grace to make any body knyght therfore/ I befeche you to make my horfe knyght & not me/ for certes it was his dede & not myne/ & full fore agaynft my will.

Whiche anfwere the kynge herynge refraynyd to promote hym to the order of knyghthode/ reputynge hym in maner but a cowarde/⁴ & euer after fauoryd hym the leffe.⁵

¶ By this tale a man may lerne how it is wyfdome for one that is in good credence to kepe hym therin/ and in nowyfe to dyfable hymfelfe to moche.

¹ *done*] Hazl. wonne.
² *becaufe that*] Hazl. becaufe.
³ *man*] orig. reads men.
⁴ *but a cowarde*] Hazl. but for a cowarde.
⁵ *the leffe*] Hazl. the leffe therfore.

LXVI. *Of the man that wold haue the pot ſtand there as he wold.*[1]

The ſame ſtory is related in the " Scole-houſe of Women," 1542; vide " Select Pieces of Early Popular Poetry," Lond. 1825, vol. ii. p. 77-78, " *All though the mete therin were not inough, ſodenly cõmaundyd her.*" Mr. Hazlitt conſiders this paſſage very corrupt: but the uſe of the word "*ynough*" in No. 92 ſhows, plainly enough, that his ſuppoſition is falſe.

YONGE man late maryed to a wyfe thowght it was good polycy to get the mayſtry of her in the begynnynge. Cam to her the pot ſethynge ouer yᵉ fyre all though the mete therin were not inough ſodenly cõmaundyd her to take the pot from the fyre. whyche anſweryd & ſayde that yᵉ mete was not redy to ete. And he ſayd agayne I wyll haue it taken of for my pleaſure. This good woman loth yet to offend hym ſet yᵉ pot beſyde the fyre as he bad.[2] And anone after he cõmaũded her to ſet the pot behynde the dore/ & ſhe ſayd therto agayne ye be not wyſe therin. But he preciſely ſayd it ſholde be ſo as he bad. And ſhe gentylly

---

[1] Hazl. Of hym that wolde gette the mayſtrye of his wyfe.   [2] *bad*] in orig. had.

agayne did his cōmaū́dement. This man yet not fatysfyed cōmaunded her to fet the pot a hygh vpon the hen roft/ what quod yᵉ wyf agayne³ I trow ye be mad. And he fyerſly than cōmaunded her to fet it there or els he ſayd ſhe ſholde repēt⁴ She ſomewhat aferde to moue⁵ his pacience toke a ladder and fet it to the rooft/ and wēt herſelf vp the ladder and toke the pot in her hande prayeng her huſbande than to holde the ladder faft for ſlydynge/ whiche ſo dyd.

And whenne the huſbande lokyd vp and ſawe the Potte ſtande there on hyght⁶ he ſayde thus. Lo now ſtandyth the pot there as I wolde haue it This wyfe herynge that fodenly pouryd the hote potage on his hed & fayd thus. And now bene the potage there as I wolde haue them.

¶ By this tale men may ſe it is no wyſedome for a man to attempte a meke womãs pacyēce to far left it torne to his owne hurte & damage.

³ *what quod the wyf agayne*] Hazl. What! quod the wyfe.
⁴ *repent*] Hazl. repent it.
⁵ *moue*] in orig. mone.
⁶ *on hyght*] orig. reads an hyght.

LXVII. *Of the penytent that ſayd the ſhepe of god haue mercy vpon me.*

In G. Wickram, "Der Rollwagen," Frankf. 1590, fol. 47, *verſo*: "Von einem einfaeltigen Bawren der da beichtet vnd kundt nicht beten," this ſtory has been amplified: until St. John's Day the penitent ſays, "the lamb of God have mercy upon me;" afterwards, "the ſheep of God;" and later in the year, about the beginning of autumn, "the wether of God." In Kirchhof, "Wendunmuth," Frankf. 1573, i. fol. 255, *verſo*: "Ein Schaefer lehrnet betten," he ſays, "the wether of God," after the prieſt has reproved him for ſaying "the ſheep of God." Item in Naſr-eddin's "Schwänke," 1857; No. 105, p. 43; cf. No. 115, p. 47.

A CERTAYNE confeſſour in the holy tyme of lente inioyned his penitent to ſay dayly for his penaunce this prayer. Agnus dei miſerere mei/ whiche was as moche to ſaye in englyſshe as yᵉ Lambe of god haue mercy vpon me. This penitens acceptynge his penaũce departyd & that tyme twelfe moneth after came agayne to be confeſſyd of the ſame cõfeſſoure whiche demaundyd of hym whether he had fulfyllyd his penaũce that he hym inioynyd yᵉ laſt yere. And he ſayd thus/ ye ſyr I thank god I haue fulfylled it/ for I haue ſayde thus to daye mornynge¹ and ſo dayly. The ſhepe of

---

¹ *mornynge*] Hazl. in the mornynge.

god haue mercy vpon me. To whom the confeſſour ſayd. Nay I bad yᵉ ſay Agnus dei miſerere mei/ that is yᵉ lambe of god haue mercy vpon me.

Ye ſyr quod yᵉ penytent ye ſay trouth that was yᵉ laſte yere/ but now it is at twelfe month[2] ſyth/ & it is a ſhepe by this tyme. Therfore I muſt nedys ſay now yᵉ ſhepe of god haue mercy vpon me.

¶ By this tale ye may perceyue that yf holy ſcrypture be expownyd to rude[3] Lay people onely in the lytterall ſcence. Peraduenture it ſhal do but lytell[4] good.

LXVIII. ¶ *Of the huſband that ſayd he was John daw.*

IT fourtuned dyuers to be in cõmunycacyon amonge whom there was a curat or a paryſh preeſt & one Johan daw a paryſhon of his whiche .ii. had cõmunycacyon more buſy than other in this maner. This preeſt thought yᵗ one myght not by felynge knowe one from another in the darke/ John

---

[2] *at twelfe month*] Hazl. a twelfemonthe.
[3] *rude*] Hazl. the.
[4] *but lyttel*] Hazl. lytell.

daw his paryſhon of contrary[1] opynyon layde with his curate for a wager .xl. pence.

Wherupon the paryſh preeſt wyllynge to proue his wager wente to this John dawes houſe in the euenynge and ſodenly gate hym to bed with his wyfe where whẽ he began to be ſomwhat beſy. She felynge his crowne ſayde ſhortly with a loud voyce. By god thou art not John daw. That herynge her huſbond anſwerde. Thou ſayſt trouth wyfe I am here John daw. Therfore mayſter perſon gyue me the money for you haue loſt your .xl. pence.

¶ By this tale ye may lerne to perceyue y^t it is no wyſdome for a man for ye couetouſe of wynnyng of any wager to put in Jeoperdy a thyng that may torne hym to gretter dyſplaſure.

LXIX. ¶ *Of the ſkoler of oxford that prouyd by ſoupheſtry .ii. chekyns .iii.*

In Ottom. Luſcinius, "Joci ac Sales, &c." 1524, No. 36, three eggs are proved to be five; ſee "Certayne Conceyts and Jeaſts," 1614, No. 32, in "Shakeſpeare Jeſt-Books," iii. p. 14; in Joh. Manlius, "Loci Communes," Baſil. 1590, p. 451, three eggs to be ſix; repeated in Joh. Pet. de Memel,

[1] *of contrary*] Hazl. of the contrary.

"Luſtige Geſellſchaft," 1695, No. 609. Cammerer, "Fabulæ Æſopicæ," Lips. 1570, p. 384, has a ſtory where two eggs are made ſix; in Gerlach, " Eutrapeliarum," lib. i. No. 871, p. 227, (Lips. 1656,) four eggs are made ſeven. Similar ſtories in Mart. Montanus, " Gartengeſellſchaft," Straſsb. s. a. 14; in "Scoggin's Jeſts," 1626, Mr. Hazlitt's reprint, p. 62; and in "Joake upon Joake," 1721. Compare Cénac Moncaut, " Contes Populaires de la Gaſcogne," Paris, 1861, p. 5; Reinh. Koehler in " Jahrbuch für Romaniſche und Engliſche Literatur," ed. by Ebert, vol. v. faſc. 1, p. 4.

A RYCH frankelyn in yᵉ contrey hauynge by his wyfe but one chyld and no mo for the grete affeccyon that he had to his ſayde chylde founde hym at Oxford to ſcole by the ſpace of .ii. or .iii. yere. This yonge ſcoller in a vocacyon tyme for his dyſport came home to his fader.

It fortuned afterwarde in[2] a nyght the fader yᵉ moder & the ſayde yonge ſcoller ſyttynge at ſupper hauynge before them no more mete but onely a cople of chykyns the fader ſayd this wyfe. Sone ſo it is that I haue ſpent moch money vpon the to fynde yᵉ to ſcole/ wherfore I haue grete deſyre to know what haſt lernyd. To whom yᵉ ſone anſwerde & ſayde. Fader I haue ſtudyed foueſtrye & by that ſcyence I can proue yᵗ theſe

[2] *in*] Hazl. on.

.ii. chykyns in yͤ dyſh be thre chykyns. Mary
ſayd yͤ fader that wolde I fayne ſe. The ſcoller
toke one of yͤ chykyns in his hand & ſayd. Lo
here is one chykyn/ and incõtynent he toke both
yͤ chykyns in his hand ioyntly & ſayd here is .ii.
chykyns and one & .ii. maketh .iii. Ergo here
is .iii. chykyns. Then the fader toke one of the
chykyns to hymſelfe and gaue another to his
wyfe & ſayd thus. Lo I wyll haue one of yͤ
chykyns to my parte/ & thy moder ſhall haue
another & bycauſe of thy good argument thou
ſhalt haue yͤ thyrde to thy ſupper/ for thou
getteyſt no more mete here at this tyme/ whiche
promyſe the fader kept & ſo the ſcoller went
without his ſupper.

¶ By this tale men may ſe that it is grete foly
to put one to ſcole to lerne any ſubtyll ſcyence
whiche hath no naturall wytte.

LXX. ¶ *Of the frere that ſtale the podyng.*

The ſame ſtory is found in Tarlton's "Jeſts and News
out of Purgatory," 1590, edited by J. O. Halliwell, Lond.
1844, (Shakeſpeare Society,) p. 82.

FRERE of london there was that on a
ſondaye mornynge yarly in yͤ ſomer
ſeaſõ came from Londõ to Barnet to

make a colacyon/[1] & was there an houre before hye maſſe began/ & bycauſe he wolde come to yᵉ chyrch honeſtly/ he went fyrſt to an alehouſe there to wype his ſhoys & to make hymſelf clenely. In the which houſe there were podyngis to ſelle/ & dyuers folkys there brekynge theyr faſte & etyng podyngys. But yᵉ frere brake his faſt in a ſecrete place in the ſame houſe.

This frere ſoone after came to the chyrch and by lycence of yᵉ curat enteryd-in to the pulpet to make a colacyon or ſermon. And in his ſermon there he rebukyd ſore yᵉ maner of them that vſyd[2] to breke theyr faſt on the ſonday before hye maſſe & ſayd it was called yᵉ dyuyls blak brekfaſt. And with that worde ſpekyng as he dyd caſt his armys out to make his cõntenaũce there fell a podynge out of his ſleue/ which he hymſelf had ſtolẽ a lytel before in yᵉ ſame alehous & when yᵉ people ſawe that & ſpecyally they yᵗ brake theyr faſt there yᵉ ſame mornyng & knew wel that yᵉ wyfe had compleyned how ſhe had one of her podynges ſtolyn/ they laughyd ſo moche at the frere yᵗ he incõtynent went downe of the pulpet[3] for ſhame.

¶ By this tale a man may ſe that whẽ a precher

---

[1] *colacyon*] i. e. homily.
[2] *vſyd*] Hazl. met.
[3] *of the pulpet*] Hazl. out of the pulpet.

doth rebuke any synne or vyce wherin he is knowē openly to be gylty hymſelf/ ſuche prechyng ſhall lytell edyfy to the people.

LXXI. *Of the frankelyns ſon that cam to take orders.*

To ſolve the ſame problem a wife aſks her huſband who had been the father of the miller's three ſons, whereupon this miller is proved to be the father of Shem, Ham, and Japheth, (Joh. Pet. de Memel, "Luſtige Geſellſchaft," 1695, 1.) In Gerlach, "Eutrapeliarum," lib. i. No. 665, p. 159, the queſtion is, who was the father of Zebedee's children, and the anſwer: our neighbour, Maſter Melcher, the miller; in "Scoggin's Jeſts," (repr. p. 68,) the ſcholar ſays, "Tom Miller of Oſeney was Jacob's father." Alſo in "Die Sutorio Magiſtrale ſeltzame Metamorphoſis (der Pedantiſche Jrrthum, &c." Rapperſweil, 1673), and in Balthaſar Schupp (Wackernagel's "Leſebuch," iii. 795.)

A very ſimilar ſtory can be heard to this day in Germany: A waiter in the Weidenbuſch Hotel in Frankfort o. M. propoſes the following riddle to a Pruſſian Lieutenant: "It is not my brother, it is not my ſiſter, and yet it is my mother's child." The lieutenant gueſſes and gueſſes, until at laſt the waiter tells him that it is he himſelf. On the following day the lieutenant puts the ſame riddle at an evening party. The whole company declares: "That is yourſelf, Lieutenant!" "No, Ladies and Gentlemen, it is the waiter at the Weidenbuſch Hotel."

CERTAYNE ſkoller ther was intendynge to be made preſt[1] whiche had nother grete wytte nor lernyng came to the byſshop to take orders/ whos folyſhneſſe yᵉ byſhop perceyuyng becauſe he was a ryche mānes ſon wolde not very ſtrongly oppoſe[2] hym but aſkyd hym this ſmall queſtyon. Noe had .iij. ſonnes/ Sem/ Cham & Japhet/ now tell me quod the byſshop wo was Japhetis father & thou ſhalt haue orders. Then ſayd yᵉ ſcoler By my trouth my lorde I pray you pardō me. For I neuer lernyd but lyttel of the byble. Then quod the byſhop/ go home & come agayn & ſoyle me this queſtyon & thou ſhalt haue orders.

This ſcoler ſo departed & came home to his fader & ſhewde hym yᵉ cauſe of the hynderaunce of his orders.

His fader beynge angry at his folyſshnes thought to teche hym yᵉ ſolucyon of this queſtyon by a famylyer example & called his ſpanyels before hym & ſayd thus/ thou knowyſt well Coll my dogge hath theſe iii. whelpys Ryg/ Tryg/ & Tryboll. Muſt not Coll my dog[3] nedys be Syre to tryboll. Then quod the ſcoler by god fader

---

[1] *preſt*] Hazl. a preeſt.
[2] *oppoſe*] in orig. appoſe.
[3] *Coll my dog*] Hazl. all my dogges.

ye saye trouth let me alone now/ ye shall se me do well ynough yᵉ nexte tyme. wherfore on yᵉ morowe he wente to yᵉ byſshop agayne & ſayd he coud ſoyle his queſtyon. Then ſayd the byſshop Noe had .iii. ſonnes Sem Cham & Japhet/ now tell me who was Japhetys fader. Mary ſyr quod yᵉ ſcoler yf it pleaſe your lordſhyp Col my faders dog.

¶ By this tale a man may lerne that it is but loſt tyme to teche a fole any thynge whych hath no wyt to perceyue it.

LXXII. *Of the huſbandman that lodgyd the frere in hys owne bed.*

IT fortuned ſo that a frere late in the euenynge deſyred lodgynge of a poore man of the countrey/ the whiche for lake of other lodgynge glad to herborowe the frere lodgyd hym in his owne bed. And after he and his wyfe. The frere beynge a ſleepe came and lay in the ſame bedde.

And in the mornynge after the poore man roſe and wente to the marketh leuynge the Frere in yᵉ bedde with his wyfe. And as he went he ſmylyd & laughyd to hymſelf/ wherfor his neybours demaunded of hym why he ſo ſmyled/ he anfwerd & fayd I laugh to thynk how fhamefaſt the frere fhall be when he waketh/ whom I left in bedde with my wyfe.

¶ By this tale a man may lerne that he that ouerfhotyth hymſelf doth folyfhly yet he is more fole to fhewe it openly.

LXXIII. *Of the preſt that wold ſay .ii. goſpels for a grote.*

A very curious inſtance of a corruption proving an edition to be a reviſion of an older text. Mr. Hazlitt reads "ſhorte ſpace," and there can be no doubt, that our reading, "ſhoterey," is the original and older one, as a village, Shottery, is ſituated, exactly as our ſtory mentions, not a mile from Stratford-on-Avon (Weſt), between this place and Bordon Hill.

SOMTYME there dwellyd a preſt in Stretforth vpon auyne of ſmall lernynge whiche vndeuoutly ſange maſſe/ & often tymes twyſe on one day. So it happened on a tyme after his fecõde mas was done in fhoterey[1] not a myle from Strethforth there mete with hym dyuers merchaunt men whiche wolde haue harde maſſe/ & defyryd hym to fynge maſſe and he ſholde haue a grote/ whiche anſwerd them

---

[1] *ſhoterey*] Hazl. ſhorte ſpace.

& fayd Syrs I wyll fay maffe no more this day/ but I wyl fay you .ii. gofpels for one grote/ & that is dog chepe a maffe in ony place in eng-londe.

¶ By this tale a man may fe that they that be rude & vnlernyd regard but lytell the meryt & goodnes of holy prayer.

LXXIV. *Of the courtear that dyd caft the frere ouer the bote.*

Too imperfect to decypher in Hazl.

A COURTYER & a frere happenyd to mete togyder in a fery bote & in cõmunycacyon betwene them fell at wordys angry & dyfpleafyd eche with other/ & fought & ftrogled togyder/ fo that at the laft ye courtyer caft the frere ouer the bote/ fo was ye frere drowned. The feryman whiche had ben a man of warre the moft parte of his lyfe before and feynge the frere was fo drowned & gon fayd thus to the courtyer/ I befhrewe thy hart thou fholdeft haue taryed & foughte with hym a lande for nowe thou haft caufed me to lefe an halfpeny for my fare.

¶ By this tale a man may fe that he yᵗ is accoftumed in vycyous & cruel company fhall lofe that noble vertew to haue pyte & compaffyon vpon his neyghboure.

LXXV. *Of the frere that prechyd what mennys fowlys were.*

A PRECHER in the pulpet¹ whiche prechyd the worde of god/ & amõg other matters fpake of mennys foullys & fayd they were fo meruelous & fo fubtyll yᵗ a thoufand foullys myght daūce in the fpace of a nayle of a mannys fynger/ amonge whiche audyence there was a mery conceyted felowe of fmall deuocyon that anfwerde and fayd thus/ mayfter doctor yf that² a thoufande foullys may daunce on a mannys nayle I pray you tell then³ where fhall the pyper ftande.

¶ By this tale a man may fe that it is but foly to fhewe or to teche vertew to them that haue no pleafure nor mynde therto.

¹ *in the pulpet*] Hazl. in pulpet.
² *yf that*] Hazl. yf.
³ *you tell then*] Hazl. you than.

LXXVI. *Of the huſband that cryed ble vnder the bed.*

This tale, the origin of which perhaps may go back to Oriental ſources, (ſee Theodor Benfey, "Pantſchatantra," Leipzig, 1859, vol. ii. p. 258,) is taken from the "Cent Nouvelles Nouvelles," nov. 4; it is repeated in Celio Maleſpini, "Ducento Novelle," nov. 15, and in "Les joyeuſes Adventures et nouvelles Récréations," Paris, 1682, p. 35, 5ᵗᵒ, devis 9.

IN londõ there was a certayn artyfycer hauyng a wyf to whõ a luſty galãt made purſute to accomplyſhe his pleaſur. This womã denyenge ſhewde the matter vnto her huſbande/ whiche mouyd therwith bad hys wyfe to appoynte hym a tyme to come ſecretly to lye with her all night. And wᵗ gret krakys & othes ſware yᵗ agaynſt his coming he wolde be redy harneſyd & wolde put hym in ieopardy of his lyf except[1] he wolde make hym a grete amendys. This nyght was then[2] appoynted at whiche tyme this courtyer came at

---

[1] *agaynſt hys coming . . . of his lyf except*] This paſſage is apparently corrupt in orig., it reads: agaynſt his lyf except coming . . . in jeopardy of his comyng, he wolde, &c.

[2] *then*] orig. reads them.

his howre & entred into the chaumber³ fet⁴ his two handfworde⁵ downe & fayde thefe wordes. Stand thou there thou fworde the deth of .iii.⁶ men.

This hufbande lyenge vnder yᵉ bed in harnes heryng thefe wordes lay ftyl for fere. The courtyer anone gat him to bed with the wyfe aboute his prepenfyd befynes/ and within an houre or .ii.⁷ the hufbande beynge wery of lyenge began to remoue hym/ the courtyar that herynge afkyd the wyfe what thynge that was yᵗ remouyd vnder yᵉ bed/ whiche excufynge yᵉ matter fayde it was a lytell fhepe that was wonte dayly to go about the hous & the hufbande yᵗ herynge anone cryed ble as it had ben a fhepe.

And fo in cōclufyon when yᵉ courtyer faw his tyme he rofe & kyffed the wyfe & toke his leue & departyd. And as foone as he was gone the hufbande arofe/ & when the wyfe lokyd on hym fomwhat abaffhyd fhe began to make a fad coū-tenaunce & fayde Alas fyr why dyd ye not ryfe & play the man as ye fayde ye wolde/ whiche anfwerde and fayde why dame dydeft thou not here hym fay that his fworde had ben the dethe

---

³ *into the chaumber*] Hazl. in at the chamber.
⁴ *fet*] Hazl. and fet.
⁵ *two handfworde*] Hazl. two-hande fworde.
⁶ *.iii.*] Hazl. thre.   ⁷ *.ii.*] Hazl. two.

of .iii. men/ & I had ben a fole than yf y^t I had put my felfe in ieopardy to haue ben the fourth. Then fayd the wyfe thus/ but fyr fpake not I wyfely then when I fayd ye were a fhepe/ yes quod ye hufbande. But than dyd not I more wyfely dame when that I cryed ble.

¶ By this ye may fe that he is not wyfe that wyll put his confydens to moche vpon thefe grete crakers whiche oftymes wyll do but lytell when it comyth to the poynt.

LXXVII. *Of the fhomaker that afkyd the colyer what tydyngys in hell.*

A correfponding tale in Lyrum Carum, 125.

THERE was a fhomaker[1] fyttynge in his fhop y^t fawe a colyer come by thought to deryde hym bycaufe he was fo blake/ afkyd[2] hym what thydynges were in hell[3] and how the deuyll fayred. To whome the colyer fayde/ the deuyll fared well[4] when

---

[1] *There was a fhomaker*] Hazl. A fouter.

[2] *afkyd*] Hazl. and afked.

[3] *what thydynges were in hell*] Hazl. what newes from hell.

[4] *fayde/ the deuyll fared well*] Hazl. anfwered hym he was well.

I sawe hym laft for he was rydynge forthe and taryed but for a fowter[5] to pluk on his botis.

¶ By this ye may fe that he that vfyth to deryde other folkys is fomtyme hymfelfe more derydyd and mokkyd.

LXXVIII. *Of feynt Peter that cryed caufe bobe.*

I FYNDE wrytē amonge olde geftys how god made faynte peter porter of heuen/ and that god of his goodnes foone after his paffyon fuffred many men to come to the kyngdome of heuen with fmall deferuyng/ at whiche tyme there was in heuen a grete company of Welchemen/ whiche with theyre krakynge & babelynge trobelyd all the other. Wherfore god fayd to faynt peter yt he was wery of them/ & that he wolde fayne haue them out of heuen. To whome faynt Peter fayde good lorde I warrant you yt fhalbe fhortly done/[6] wherfore faynt peter went out of heuē gatys & cryed wt a loude voyce Caufe bobe/ yt is as moche to fay as roftyd chefe/ whiche thynge ye welchmen heryng ran out of heuyn a great pace. And when faynt Peter fawe them al out he fodenly went in to

[5] *fowter*] i.e. cobbler.   [6] *fhortly done*] Hazl. done.

heuen and lokkyd the dore and so sparryd all the
welchmen out.

⁋ By this ye may se that it is no wysdome for
a man to loue or to set his mynde to moche vpon
ony delycate or wordly pleasure wherby he shall
lose the celestyall & eternall Joye.

LXXIX. *Of hym that aduenturyd body & sowle
for hys prynce.*

TWO knyghtes there were whiche went
to a stondyng felde wᵗ theyr prynce.
But one of them was cõfessyd before
he went/ but the other wēt into the felde w'out
shryft or repētaūce/ afterward this price wã yᵉ
feld & had yᵉ vyctorye yᵗ day/ wherfore he yᵗ was
cõfessyd came to yᵉ price & askyd an offyce &
sayd he had deseruyd¹ it for he had don good
seruyce & aduētured that day as far as ony man
in yᵉ felde/ to whõ the other yᵗ was vncõfessyd
answeryd and sayd nay by the mas I am more
worthy to haue a rewarde than he/ for he aduenturyd but his body for your sake for he durst
not go to yᵉ felde tyl he was cõfessyd/ but as for

---

¹ *he had deseruyd*] Hazl. that he had deserved.

me I dyd iupd both body lyfe & foule for your fake/ for I went to the felde without cõfeffyon or repentañce.

LXXX. *Of the parſon that ſtall the mylners elys.*

Too imperfect to decypher in Hazl.
In Reginald Scot, "Difcovery of Witchcraft," 1584, London, 1651, 4to. p. 191, the fame ſtory is related.

A CERTAYN mylner ther was which had dyuers põdys of elis wherĩ was good ſtore of elys/ wherfore ye pſon of ye town which lokyd like ã holy mã dyuers & many timis ſtale many of thẽ in ſo moch y^t he had left few or none behind him/ wherfore this milner feyng his elis ſtolyn & wiſt not by whõ cam to ye fayd pſon & defyrid[2] hym to curfe for thẽ ye pſon fayd he wolde. & ye next sõday cã in to ye pulpet w^t book bell & cãdell & pcei-yng there were none in ye chirche y^t vnderſtode latyn fayd thus/ he y^t ſtale ye milners elis laudate dominum de celis but he y^t ſtale ye grer elis gaudeat ipfe in celis/ therw^t put out ye candell. why[3] fyr quod ye mylner no more for this fauce is ſharp ynough for hym.

[2] *defyrid*] in orig. deſtrid.   [3] *why*] in orig. who.

¶ By this ye may fe that fome curatys that loke full holyly be but defemblers & ypocrytis.

LXXXI. *Of the welchman that faw one .xl. fhyl. better than god.*

A WELCHMAN on a tyme went to chirche to here mas whiche hapenyd to come in euyn at yᵉ facryng time when he had hard yᵗ mas to yᵉ ende he wẽt home wher one of his felowes afkyd hym whether he had fene god almighty to day which ãfwerd & fayd nay but I faw one lx. s. better thã he.

¶ By this ye maye fe that they be euyll brought vp haue but lytyll devocyon to pray and vertew.[1]

LXXXII. *Of the frere that fayd dyrige for the hoggys fowle.*

A correfponding tale is found in the "Nouveaux Contes à rire," &c. Cologne, 1702, p. 13: "Cochon adroitement volé par des Bohémiens," where a family of thieves fteal a hog, kill it, and upon fearch being made for it, cover it with a cloth and weep as for their father.

[1] The moral is wanting in Hazl.

UPON a tyme certayn women in the countrey were appoynted to deryde and mokke a frere a lymytour that vſyd moche to vyſyth them. wherupon one of them a lytyll before that[2] the frere came kylled an hog & for dyſport leyd[3] it vnder the borde after the maner of a corſe and tolde the frere it was her good mã and defyred hym to ſay dirige for his ſoule wherfore the frere and his felaw began Placebo and Dirige and ſo forth ſayd the ſeruyſe full deuowtly which the wyues ſo heryng/ coude not refrayne them ſelfe from lawghynge and wente in to a lytyll parler to lawgh more at theyr pleſure. Theſe frerys ſomwhat ſuſpected the cauſe and quykly or that yᵘ women were ware lokyd vnder the borde and ſpyed that it was an hog/ ſodenly toke it bytwene them and bare it homeward as faſt they myght.[4] The women ſeyng that ran after the frere and cryed come agayn mayſter frere come agayne and let it allone/ nay by my fayth quod yᵉ frere he is a broder of oures and therfore he muſt nedys be buryed in our cloyſter/ and ſo the frerys gate the hog.

[2] *before that*] Hazl. before.
[3] *leyd*] in orig. ſeyd.
[4] *as faſt they myght*] Hazl. as faſt as they might.

¶ By this ye may fe that they that vfe to deryde and mok other fomtyme it tornyth to theyr one loffe and damage.

LXXXIII. *Of the parfon that fayd maffe of requiē for Cryftys fowle.*

This tale is taken from Henr. Bebelii, "Facetiæ, Opufcula," s. l. & a. 4to. fign. A a 4, "Fabula," (or in Frifchlini, "Facet." i. No. 7, p. 37, "De infcitia cuiusdam facerdotis fabula perfaceta"): "Nefciebat quidam facerdos fatis infulfus, quid effet cantandum in officio diuino die refurrectionis chriftianæ, mifit itaque ædituum ad vicinum facerdotem, qui cum dixiffet, Refurrexi, ædituus literarum ignarus, tantum meminit re, quod fæpius repetiuit, quo audito facerdos ille fimplex et rudis, bene eft, dixit requiem cantandum eft, quoniam diem depofitionis (vt vocant) Jefu Chrifti celebrari convenit, nam in triduo mortuus eft."

It is repeated in " Der Wegkürzer, das dritte theil des Rollwagens," &c. Frankf. 1590, fol. 15 *verfo;* and in "Scoggin's Jefts," 1626, p. 74, (repr. 1864, p. 75,) "How the Prieft faid *Requiem æternam* on Eafter day."

A CERTAYNE preft there was that dwellyd in yᵉ coūtery which was not very[1] lernyd. Therfore on Eefter euyn he fet his boy to yᵉ preft of the next town

[1] *very*] Hazl. very well.

yᵗ was .ii. myle from thens to know what maſſe he ſholde ſynge on yᵉ morowe. This boy came to the ſayd preſt and did his mayſters errāde to hym. Then quod the preſt tel thy mayſter that he muſt ſynge to morow of the reſurrexyon/ and furthermore quod he yf thou hap to forget it tel thy mayſter that it begynneth wᵗ a gret R. and ſhewed hym the maſſe booke where it was wryten Reſurrexi. &c. This boy than wente home agayne and all the way as he went he clateryd ſtyll. Reſurrexi Reſurrexi/ but at yᵉ laſt he hap‐enyd to forget it clene and whē he came home his mayſter aſkyd hym what maſſe he ſholde fynge on yᵉ morowe. By my troth mayſter quod the boy I haue forgoten it/ but he bad me tell you it begā wᵗ a gret .R. By god quod the preſt I trowe thou ſayeſt trowth for now I re‐member well it muſte be requiem eternam/ for god almyghty dyed as on yeſter day² & now we muſt ſay maſſe for his ſoule.

¶ By this ye may ſe that when one fole ſendyth another fole on his errand oftentymes the beſynes is folyſhly³ ſpede.

---

² *as on yeſter day*] Hazl. upon Good Fryday.
³ *is folyſhly*] Hazl. folyhly.

LXXXIV. *Of the herdman that sayd ryde apace ye shall haue rayn.*

In "Joe Miller's complete Jest Book," London, 1845, No. 425, p. 128, the same story is told of Newton. See "Scoggin's Jests," 1796, p. 47: "How Scogin gave a Cowheard forty shillings to teach him his cunning in the weather." Mr. Hazlitt's reprint, p. 115.

SKOLER of Oxenford whiche had studyed y^e iudycyals of astronomy õ a tyme was rydyng by y^e way which cā by a herdmã & inquyrid of hym how far it was to y^e next town/ syr quod y^e herdmã ye haue notthyder past a myle & ã half/ but syr quod he ye nede to ryde apace for ye shal haue a shour of rayn er ye cõe thyder/ what quod ye skoler y^t is not so for here is no token of rayn for all[1] ye cloudys be both fayr & clere/ by god syr quod ye herd mã but ye shall fynd it so. The skoler then rode forth his way & or he had ryden half a myle forther there fel a good showre of rayn that the skoler was well wasshyd and wete to ye skyn/ ye skoler then tournyd his horse and rode agayne[2] to the herdman & desyred hym to teche hym that connyng. nay quod ye herdman I wyll

---

[1] *for all*] Hazl. for. [2] *rode agayne*] Hazl. rode.

not teche you my connynge for nought/ thā the
ſkoler profferyd hym .xl. ſhyllyngys to teche hym
that connynge/ the herde man after he had re-
ceyued his money ſayde thus. Syr ſe you not yõder
dun a kow³ with the whyte face/ yes quod the
ſkoler. Suerly quod yᵉ herdmā whē ſhe daūſyth
and holdyth vp her tayle it ſhal haue a ſhowre of
rayne within halfe an howre after.

¶ By this ye may ſee yᵗ the cõnyng of herdmen⁴
& ſhepardes as touchyng alteracyõs of weders
is more ſure than yᵉ iudycyallys of Aſtronomy.

LXXXV. *Of hym that ſayd I ſhall haue nere a peny.*

IN a certayn town ther was a rych man
that lay on his deth bed at poynte of
deth whiche chargyd his executours
to dele⁵ for his ſoule a certayn ſōme of money
in pence & on this condicyon chargyd them as
yᵉ wolde anſwere afore God⁶ that euery pore
man that came to them & tolde a trewe tale
ſholde haue a peny & they that ſayd a fals

---

³ *kow*] Hazl. ewe.
⁴ *herdmen*] orig. reads herdman.
⁵ *to dele*] i. e. to give.
⁶ *afore God*] in orig. afore. God

thynge sholde haue none/ & in the dole¹ tyme there came one which sayde yᵗ god was a good man/ quod yᵉ executours thou shalt haue a peny for thou sayste trouth. Anone came another & said yᵉ deuyll was a good man/ quod the executours there thou lyest therfore thou shalt haue nere a peny. At last came one to yᵉ executours & sayd thus/ ye shall gyue me nere a peny/ which wordys made the executours amasyd and toke aduysement whether they shold gyue hym the peny or no.

¶ By this ye may se it is wysdome for Juggys in deutefull matters of law to beware of hasty iugement.

LXXXVI. *Of the husband that sayd his wyfe and he agreed well.*

Too imperfect to decypher in Hazl.

MAN askyd his neybour which was but late maryed to a wydow how he agreyd with his wyfe for he said yᵗ her fyrst husbād and she coud neuer agre/ by god quod yᵉ other we agre meruelous wel. I pray the how so/ mary quod yᵉ other I shall tell yᵉ/

---

¹ *dole*] i.e. grief.

when I am mery fhe is mery/ & when I am fad fhe is fad/ for whē I go out of my doris I am mery to go from her & fo is fhe/ & when I come in agayne I am fad & fo is fhe.

LXXXVII. *Of the preeſt that ſayd comede epiſcope.*

From the " Margarita Facetiarum," Argent. 152, ſign. O vi.

Another verſion of this tale is related in " Scoggin's Jeſts:" How the Prieſt was complained on for keeping a young wench in his houſe," (repr. 1864, p. 78.)

IN yᵉ tyme of vyſytacyõ a bysſhop whiche was ſomwhat lecherous & had got many chylderne preparyd to come to a preſtes houſe to ſe[2] what rule he kept which preſt had a lemã in his houſe called Ede & by her had .ii. or .iii. ſmale chyldrē in ſhort ſpace/ but agayn yᵉ bysſhop commyng yᵉ preſt[3] preparyd a rome to hyde his lemã & his childrē ouer in yᵉ rofe of his hall/ & whē yᵉ bysſhop was come & ſet at dyner in yᵉ ſame hal hauyng .x. of his owne childrē about hym this preſte which coud ſpeke lytell latyn or none bad the bysſhop in

---

[2] *to come to a preſtes houſe to ſe*] Hazl. to queſtion a preeſt.

[3] *the preſt*] Hazl. he.

latyn to ete faynge Comede epifcope. This
womã in the rofe of the houfe herynge the preſt
fay fo had wente he had callyd her byddynge her
com Edee & ãfwerd fhortly & fayd fhall I brynge
my chylderen wᵗ me alfo. This bysfhop herynge
this¹ vxor tua ficut vitis abundans in lateribus
domus tue. The preeſt thẽ half amafyd anfweryd
fhortly² and fayd Filii tui ficut nouelle³ olyuarum
in circuitu menfe tue.

¶ By this ye may fe that they that haue but
fmall lernynge fomtyme fpeke truely vnaduyfyd.

LXXXVIII. *Of the woman that ſtale the pot.*

ON afhe wednyfday in yᵉ mornynge was
a curat of a church whiche had made
good chere the nyght afore/ & fyttyn
vp late & came to yᵉ churche to here cõfeſſyon
to whom there came a woman/ and amõge other
thyngys fhe cõfeſſyd her that fhe had ſtolyn a
pot. But than becaufe of grete watche that this
preeſt had/ he there fodenly felle a flepe/ and
whẽ this woman fawe hym not wyllyng to here
her fhe rofe vp⁴ & wẽt her way/ & anone an

---

¹ *herynge this*] Hazl. hering this, fayde in fporte.
² *anfweryd fhortly*] Hazl. anfwerd.
³ *nouelli*] orig. reads nouelle.
⁴ *rofe vp*] Hazl. rofe.

other woman kneled downe to the same prest & began to say benedicite wherwith this preest sodenly wakyd wenynge⁵ she had ben the other woman & sayd al angerly/ what art thou now at benedicite agayne tell me what dydest thou when thou hadyst stolyn the pot.

LXXXIX. *Of master whyttyntons dreme.*

SONE after one mayster Whyttintõ had bylded a colege on a nyght as he slept he dremyd that he sad in his church & many folkys ther also/ & further he dremyd yᵗ he sawe our lady in the same chyrch wᵗ a glas of goodly oyntement in her hand goynge to one askyng hym what he had done for her sake/ whiche sayd that he had sayd our ladys sauter⁶ euery day wherfore she gaue hym a lytyll of the oyle. And anon she went⁷ to another askyng hym what he had done for her sake which sayd that he had sayd .ii. ladys sauters euery day/ wherfore our lady gaue hym more of yᵉ oỹtement than she gaue yᵉ other. This mayster whyttentõ

---

⁵ *wakyd wenynge*] Hazl. awaked, and wenynge.
⁶ *sauter*] i.e. Psalter.
⁷ *she went*] in orig. se went.

then thought that when our lady fholde come to hym fhe wolde gyue hym all the hole glas bycaufe y*t* he had bylded fuch a gret colege & was very glad in his mynd. But whē our lady cam to hym fhe afked hym what he had fuffred for her fake/ which wordys made hym gretly abafhyd bycaufe he had nothyng to fay for hym felfe/ & fo he dremyd[1] that for all the gret dede of byldyng of y*e* fayd Colege he had no parte of y*t* goodly oyntement.

¶ By this ye may[2] fe that to fuffer for goddys fake is more merytoryous than to gyue gret goodys.

xc. *Of the preft that kyllyd hys horfe callyd modicum.*

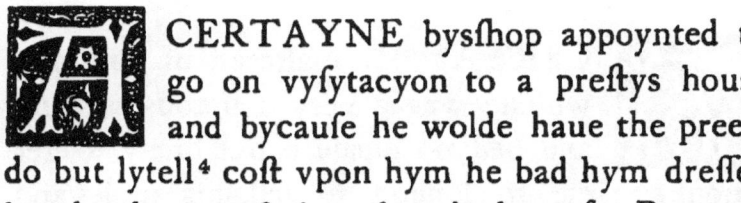CERTAYNE bysfhop appoynted to go on vyfytacyon to a preftys hous[3] and bycaufe he wolde haue the preeft do but lytell[4] coft vpon hym he bad hym dreffe[5] but lytyl mete faying thus in latyn.[6] Preparas

[1] *he dremyd*] Hazl. him informed.
[2] *may*] orig. reads mnay.
[3] *preftys hous*] Hazl. preefte's.
[4] *lytell*] in orig. lyiell.
[5] *bad hym dreffe*] Hazl. told him to prepare.
[6] *thus in latyn*] Hazl. thus.

mihi modicū. This preeſt which vnderſtode hym not halfe wel had a horſe called modicū wherfore he thought to obtayne the bysſhops fauour & agaynſt yᵉ bysſhops comyng kylled his horſe that was called modicum wherof the byſſop & his feruātes ete p̃t which whē yᵉ bisſhop knew afterward was gretly diſpleſid.

¶ By this ye may ſe that many a fole doth moche coſt which⁷ hath but lytyll thank for his laboure.

XCI. *Of the maltman of Colbroke.*

Wanting in Hazl.
Similar trickeries are of very frequent occurrence; ſee f. i. Kirchhof, "Wendunmuth," Frankf. 1573, No. 313-17, fol. 302 *verſo*.

CERTAYNE maltman of colbroke whiche was a very couetous wreche and had no pleaſure but onely to get money came to london to ſell his malt and broughte with hym .iiii. capons & there re- ſeyuyd .iiii. or .v. li. for malte and put it in a lytell purs tyed to his cote and after wente aboute the ſtrettys to ſell his capons whom a pollyng

---

⁷ *which*] Hazl. at dyners, whiche.

felowe that was a dycer and an vnthryft had
efpyed and Imagyned how he myght begyle the
man other of his capons or of his money and
came to this maltman in the ftreet berynge thefe
capons in his hande and afkyd hym how he wolde
fell his capons and when he had fhewyd hym the
pryfe of them he bad hym go with hym to his
mayfter and he wolde fhew them to his mayfter
and he wolde caufe hym to haue money for them
wherto he agreed. This Poller wente to the
cardynalls hat in lomberdys ftrete & when he
came to the dore he toke the capons from the
maltman and bad hym tary at the dore tyll he
had fhewed his mayfter and he wolde come agayn
to hym and brynge hym his money for them.
This poller when he had goten the capons wente
in to the houfe and wente thorowe the other bak
entre in to Cornhyll and foo toke the capons with
hym/ and when this maltman had ftond there a
good feafon he afkid one of the tauerners where
the man was that had the Capons to fhewe to
his mayfter/ mary quod the tauerner I can not
tell the here is nother mayfter nor man in this
houfe for this entre here is a comen hye way and
gooth in to cornhyl/ I am fure he is gone a weye
with thy capõs. This maltman herynge that ran
throwe the entre in to cornhyll and afkyd for a
felowe in a tawny cote that had capons in his

hand. But no man coude tell hym whiche waye
he was gone and foo the maltman lofte his capons
and after wente in to his Inne all heuy and fade
and toke his horfe to thentent to ryde home.
This poller by that tyme had chaungyd hys rayment and borowyd a furryd gowne and came to
the maltman fyttynge on horfbak and fayd thus/
good man me thought I harde the inquire euyn
now for one in a tawny cote that had ftolyn from
the .iiii. capõs yf thou wylt gyue me a quart of
wyne go with me and I fhall brynge yᵉ to a place
where he fyttyth drynkyng with other felowes
& had yᵉ capons in his hande. This maltman
beynge glad therof graũtyd hym to gyue hym
the wyne bycaufe he femyd to be an honeft man/
and went wᵗ hym vnto the dagger in chepe.
This poller then fayd to hym go thy way ftreyght
to thend of yᵗ long entre & there thou fhalt fe
whether it be he or no & I wyl holde thy horfe
here tyll thou come agayn. This maltman
thynkyng to fynde the felow with his capõs
wẽt in & left his horfe with the other at the
dore. And as foone as he was gon in to the
houfe this poller lad the horfe awaye in to his
owne lodgynge. This maltman inqueryd in the
houfe for his felowe with the capons but no man
coude tell hym no tydyngys of fuche man/ wherfore he came agayne to yᵉ dore all fad & lokyd

for hym yᵗ had his hors to kepe/ & bycaufe he
fawe hym not he afkyd dyuers there for hym/ &
fome fayd they faw hym & fome fayde they faw
hym not/ but no man coude tell whiche waye
he was gone wherfore he wente home to his
Inne more fad thã he was before/ wherfore his
hoft gaue hym coũcell to get hym home & beware how he truftyd any men in londõ. This
maltman feynge none other cõfort went hys hy
way homewarde.

This poller which lyngeryd alway there aboute
the Inne hard tell that the maltman was goyng
homewarde a fote apparelyd hym lyke a mannys
prentyfe & gat a lytell boget ftuffyd full of ftones
on his bake & wente before hym to charynge
croffe & taryed tyll yᵉ maltman came/ & afkyd
hym whether he wente whiche fayd to Colbroke.
Mary quod yᵉ other I am glad therof for I muft goo
to braynforde to my mayfter to bere hym money
which I haue in my boget & I wolde be glad of
cõpany. This maltman bycaufe of his owne money
was glad of his cõpany/ & fo they agreed & wente
togyder a whyle. At the laft this poller went
fomwhat before to knyghtbryge & fat vpon yᵉ
brydge & reftyd hym with his boget on his bak/
& when he faw yᵉ maltmã almoft at hym he let
his boget fall ouer yᵉ brydge in to yᵉ water. &
incontynent ftart vp & fayd to yᵉ maltman alas

I haue let my boget fal in to ye water & there is .xl. li. of money therin/ yf thou wylt wade in to ye water & go feke it & get it me agayne I fhall gyue y^e .xii. pence for thy labour/ this maltman hauynge pyte of his loffe & alfo glad to get the .xii. pence plukyd of his hofe cote & fhyrt & wadyd into ye water to feke for the boget. And in ye mene whyle this poller gote his clothis & cote wher to the purs of money was tyde & lepte ouer the hedge & wente to weftmynfter.

This maltman within a whyle after with grete payne & depe wadynge founde ye boget & came out of the water & fawe not his felowe there & fawe that his clothys & money were not there as he left them fufpectyd ye mater and openyd the boget and than founde nothynge therin but ftonys cryed out lyke a mad man and ran all nakyd to london agayne and fayde alas alas helpe or I fhall be ftolen. For my capons be ftolen. My hors is ftolen. My money and clothys be ftolen and I fhall be ftolen myfelf. And fo ran aboute the ftretys in london nakyd & mad cryenge alway I fhall be ftole. I fhall be ftolen. And fo contynuyd mad durynge his lyfe & fo dyed lyke a wretche to the vtter dyftruccyon of hym felf & fhame to all his kyn.

¶ By this tale ye may fe that many a couet- oufe wrech y^t louyd his good better than god and fettyth his mynde inordynatly theron by the ryghte iugment of god oftymes comyth to a myferable and fhamfull ende.

xcii. *Of the welchman that ftale the englyfh-mans cok.*

A WELCHEMAN dwellynge in eng-londe fortuned to ftele an englyfth mans cok & fette it on ye fyre to feth wherfore this englyfhman fufpectyng ye welchmã cam in to his houfe¹ & fawe ye cok fetyng on ye fyre & fayd to ye welchmã thus. Syr this is my cok. Mary quod ye welchmã & yf it be thyne ye fhalt haue thy parte of it/ nay quod ye eng-lyfhmã yt is not ynough. By cottes blut & her nayle quod ye welchmã yf her be not ynough now her wyll be ynough anone for her hath a good fyre vnder her.

xciii. *Of hym that brought a botell to a preft.*

CERTAYNE of ye vycars² of poulys dyfpofyd to be mery on a fondaye at hye maffe tyme fent another mad felowe

---

¹ *in to his houfe*] Hazl. to his houfe.
² *of the vycars*] Hazl. vycars.

of theyr accoyntaūce vnto a folysſhe dronken
preſte to gyue hym a botell/ whiche man met
with the preſte vpon the top of yᵉ ſtayrys by yᵉ
chaūcell dore & ſpake to hym & ſayde thus. Syr
my mayſter hath ſend you a botel to put your
drynke in bycauſe ye can³ kepe none in your
braynes. This preſte therwith beyng very angry
all ſodenly toke the botell & with his fote flange⁴
it downe into yᵉ body of the chyrche vpon the
gentylmens hedes.

XCIV. *Of the endytemēt of Jheſu of Nazareth.*

CERTAYNE Jury in the counte of
Myddelſex was inpaneld for yᵉ kynge
to inquere of all indytementes murders
& felonyes. The perſons of this panel were
folyſhe couetous & vnlerned/ for who ſo euer
wolde gyue thē a grote they wolde aſſyne &
veryfy his byll whether it were true or fals wᵗ out
any other profe⁵ or euidēce/ wherfore one yᵗ was
a mery cōceytyd felowe perceyuyng theyr ſmale
cōcyence & grete couetouſnes put in a byll in-
tytuled after this maner. Inquiratur pro dño regi

³ *ye can*] Hazl. he can.
⁴ *flange*] i. e. project out.
⁵ *any other profe*] Hazl. any profe.

ſi Jeſus nazarenus furatus eſt unū aſinū ad equitandum in egiptū/ & gaue thē a grote and deſyryd yᵗ it myght be veryfyed. The ſayd Jury whiche loked all on the grote & nothyng on yᵉ byll as was theyr vſe wrote billa vera on yᵉ bak therof which byll when it was preſentyd into yᵉ court whē yᵉ Jugys loked theron they ſayd opēly before all yᵉ people lo ſyrs here is yᵉ merueloufſt verdyt yᵗ euer was preſentyd by any[1] inqueſt for here they haue indyted Jeſu of Nazareth for ſtelyng of an aſſe which whē yᵉ people hard it/ it made thē both to laugh & to wōder at yᵉ folyſhnes & ſhāful piuri of thē of the equeſte.

¶ By this ye may ſe it is grete parell to enpanell any iurorous[2] vpon any equeſt whiche be folyſh & haue but ſmall concyence.

xcv. *Of hym that prechyd agaynſt theym that rode on the ſonday.*

The ſame ſtory is found in Friſchlini, "Facetiæ," Lips. 1600 (or 1602), p. 2, De ſacerdote jeiunium Quadrageſimale defendente : " Quidam ineptus, ne dicam impius Sacerdos, cum jeiunium Quadrageſimale et diſcrimen ciborum defenderet, et pœnam omnibus contemptoribus et hæreticis comminatus eſſet, ad erroris ſui patrocinium etiam

---

[1] *any*] Hazl. an.
[2] *iurorous*] orig. reads iurroous.

Chrifti et Apoftolorum exemplo abutebatur. Quid enim, inquit, de Chrifto et Apoftolis eius dicam ? qui nefcio qua voluptate deliniti, cum pafchatis fefto non expectato, die Jouis proxime antecedente, agnum deuoraffent, Chriftus ftatim altera poft die in crucem actus eft: Apoftolorum vero, qui vna comederant, nemo ficca morte perijt."

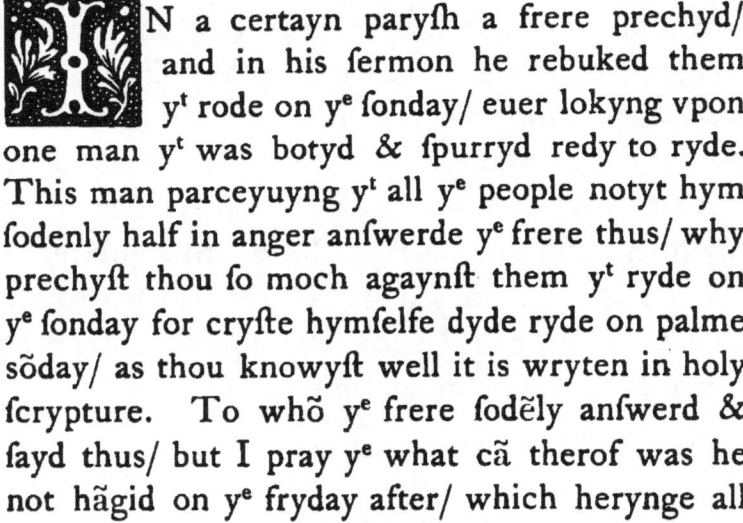IN a certayn paryſh a frere prechyd/ and in his ſermon he rebuked them y^t rode on y^e ſonday/ euer lokyng vpon one man y^t was botyd & ſpurryd redy to ryde. This man parceyuyng y^t all y^e people notyt hym ſodenly half in anger anſwerde ye frere thus/ why prechyſt thou ſo moch agaynſt them y^t ryde on y^e ſonday for cryſte hymſelfe dyde ryde on palme sõday/ as thou knowyſt well it is wryten in holy ſcrypture. To whõ ye frere ſodẽly anſwerd & ſayd thus/ but I pray ye what cã therof was he not hãgid on ye fryday after/ which herynge all ye people in ye church fell on laughing.

XCVI. *Of the one brother that founde a purs.*

Repeated in "Joe Miller's Complete Jeſt Book," London, 1845, No. 671, p. 205; and in Joh. Val. Meidinger, " Pract. Franzœſiſche Grammatik," 23rd edit. (1818), p. 551. Comp. " Waldis, Æſopus," 4, 4.

THERE was a certayne man that had two fonnys vnlyke of condycyons. For the eldyſt was luſty and quyk and vſyd moche to ryſe erly and walke in to the feldys/ than was the yonger ſlowe and vnluſty and vſyd to lye in bed¹ as longe as he myght. So on a daye the elder as he was wonte roſe erly and walkyd in to the feldys and there by fortune he founde a purs of money and brought it home to his fader. His fader when he had it wente ſtreyght to his other ſone yet lyenge then in his bed & ſayd to hym. O thou ſlogarde quod he ſeyſt thou not thyne elder² broder how he by his erly ryſyng had found a purs with money whereby we ſhalby gretely holpen all oure lyfe/ whyle thou ſluggynge in thy bed doſt³ no good but ſlepe. He then wyſt not what to ſay but anſweryd ſhortly and ſayd fader quod he yf he that hath loſt the purs and money had lyne in his bed that ſame tyme that he loſt it as I do now my broder had founde no purs nor money to daye.

¶ By this ye may ſe that they that be accuſtomyd in vyce and ſyn wyl alway fynd one excuſe or other to cloke there with theyr vyce and vnthryftynes.

---

¹ *in bed*] Hazl. in his bed.   ² *elder*] Hazl. eldeſt.
³ *doſt*] Hazl. doſt thou.

XCVII. *Of the anfwere of the masters to the mayd.*

A CERTAYN wyfe ther was whiche was fomwhat fayre and as all women be yt be ye fayre⁴ was fomwhat proude of her bewty/ & as fhe and her mayd fat togeder fhe as one that was defyrous to be preyfyd fayd to her thus. I fayth Jone how tynkyft thou am I not a fayre wyfe/ yes by my trouth mayftres quod fhe ye be the fayreft that euer was except our lady/ why by Cryft quod ye mayftres though our lady were good yet fhe was not fo fayre as men fpeke of.

¶ By this ye may fe it is harde to fynde a bewtyoufe woman without pryde.

XCVIII. *Of a certayn aldermans dedys of london.*

Wanting in Hazl.

A CERTAYNE alderman of London there was lately dyfceafed whiche now fhall be nameles whiche was very couetoufe as well before he was maryed as after/ for when he was bacheler euer when his hofen were

⁴ *the fayre*] Hazl. fayre.

broken ſo that he coude were them no longer for ſhame then wolde he cutte them of by the knee and putte on a payre of ledder buſkyns on his bare leggys whiche wolde laſte hym a two or thre yere. Furthermore it was his maner when he was a bacheler euery nyght where that he was to borowe a candels ende to brynge hym home whiche he wolde alway put in a cheſt that he had at his chamber. So that by that tyme he was maryed/ he had a cheſte of candels endis that wayd two or thre hondred weyghte.

Sone after that he was maryed to a ryche wydowe and than folkys thought he wolde be better than he was before. But ſo it happenyd that a gentylman gaue hym a paſty of an harte whiche euery day he cauſed to be ſette on the table for ſeruyce/ how be it he wolde neuer for nygynſhyp let it be openyd/ ſo that it was a moneth or vi. wekys or euer it was touched. At whiche tyme it fortuned a man of his ac-coynetaunce beynge there often and ſeynge this paſty neuer to be openyd ſayde ſyr by my trouth I wyll tame your paſty/ whiche openyd ye paſty and incontynent lepte out .iii. or .iiii. myce vpon other gentylmens trēchows whiche had crept in at an hole vndernethe the bottam and hadde etyn vp all the mete therin. Alſo this alderman was of ſuche condycyon y^t he wolde here .ii. or .iii.

massys euery daye/ and whan any pore folke came to begge of hym he wolde rebuke them and say that they dyde lette hym in heryng of them so that he wolde neuer gyue peny in almys. And on a tyme as he sat at saynt Thomas of Acres herynge masse he sawe a yonge begynner a dettour of his that owyd hym .xx. li. whiche as sone as he sawe hym he commaunded one of his seruauntes to get a sergyaunt & to arest hym whiche yonge man immedyatly after was arestyd/ and whan he was in the counter he desyred dyuers of his frendys to intrete with this Aldermā for dayes of payment whiche men in the mornynge after came to this Alderman knelynge at masse & intretyd hym for this man desyrynge hym to take dayes of paymēt whiche answeryd them thus. I praye you troble me not now for I haue harde one masse all redy & I wyll here an other or I medle with worldly matters. But yf ye haue the money here I wyll take the now or elles I pray you speke to me no more/ and so these men coude get no other answer. And this Alderman kept this yonge man styll in pryson tyll at the laste he there dyed. And so he causyd lykewyse dyuers other to dye in pryson and wolde neuer forgyue them/ wherfore afterward this alderman dyed sodenly wherfore dyuers & many were glad of his deth.

XCIX. *Of the northern man that was all hart.*

NORTHEN man there was whiche wente to feke hym a feruyce. So it happenyd that he came to a lordys place whiche lord than had war wᵗ another lord. This lord thã afkyd this northẽ mã yf yᵗ he durſt fyght/ ye by goodys byẽs quod yᵉ northẽ mã yᵗ I dare for I is al hart. whervpon the lorde retayned hym in to his feruyce. So after it happenyd yᵗ this lorde fholde go fyght with his enmyes wᵗ whom alfo wẽt this northẽ man which fhortly was fmytẽ in yᵉ hele wᵗ an arow wherfore he incõtynẽtly fell downe almoſt dede wherfore one of his felaws fayd art thou he yᵗ art all hart and for fo lytyll a ſtroke in the hele now art almoſt dede. To whom he anfweryd & fayd by goddes fale I is hard hed/ leggys/ body helys & all/ therfore ought not one to fere when he is ſtryken in yᵉ hart.

C. *Of the burnyng of old Johñ.*

The fame ſtory is related in Kirchhof, "Wendunmuth," Frankf. 1573, No. 348, fol. 333 *verfo*, "Von einem hülzern Johannes;" and in C. F. Gellert's "Fabeln," buch iii. "Die Wittwe," Leipzig, 1836, p. 165.

IN a certayn towne there was a wyfe ſomwhat agyd that had beryed her huſband whoſe name was callyd Johñ/[1] whom ſhe loued ſo tenderly in his lyfe that after his deth ſhe cauſyd an ymage of tymber to be made in vſage and perſon as lyke to hym as coude be/ whiche ymage all day longe lay vnder her bed and euery nyght ſhe cauſyd her mayde to wrap it in a ſhete & lay it in her bed & callyd it olde Johñ. This wyfe alſo had a prētyſe whoſe name was Johñ/ whiche John wolde fayn haue weddyd his mayſtres not for no grete pleaſur but onely for her good bycauſe ſhe was rych/ wherfor he imaginyd how he might obtayn his purpoſe & ſpake to yᵉ mayde of yᵉ hous & deſyryd her to lay hym in his mayſtres bed for one nyght in ſtede of the pycture/ & promyſed her a rewarde for her laboure/ which mayd ouer nyght wrappyd yᵉ ſayd yōg mā in a ſhete & layd hym in his mayſtres bed as ſhe was wōt to lay yᵉ pycture.

This wydow was wont euery nyght before ſhe ſlept & dyuers tymes whē ſhe wakyd to kys the ſayd pycture of old Johñ/ wherfore yᵉ ſayd nyght ſhe kyſſyd yᵉ ſayd yong mā beleuyng that ſhe had kyſt yᵉ pycture/ & he ſodēly ſtart & toke her in his armys and ſo well pleſed her then/ that olde

---

[1] *was callyd John*] Hazl. was John.

Johñ from thēs forth was clene out of her mynde & was cōtent yᵗ this yonge Johñ fholde lye wᵗ her ftyll all yᵗ nyght &. yᵉ pycture of olde John fholde lye ftyl vnder yᵉ bed for a thyng of nought. After this in yᵉ mornynge this wydow intendyng to plefe this yōg Johñ which had made her fo good paftyme all the nyght bad her mayd go dreffe fome good mete for theyr brekefaft to feft therwith her yōg Johñ/ this mayd whā fhe had lōge fought for wood to dres yᵉ fayd mete told her maftres yᵗ fhe coud fynd no wood yᵗ was dry except onely yᵉ picture of old Johñ yᵗ lyeth vnder yᵉ bed/ thē quod yᵉ wyf agayn/ fath[1] hym down & lay hym on yᵉ fyre for I fe well he wyll neuer do me good nor he wyll neuer do better feruyce though I kepe hym neuer fo longe. So the mayd by her cōmaundemēt dreffid yᵉ brekfaft/ & fo olde Johñ was caft out for nought & brent & from thens forth yong Johñ occupyed his place.

¶ By this tale ye may fe it is no wyfdome for a mā to kepe longe or to chyryfhe that thyng yᵗ is able to do no pleafure nor feruyce.[2]

[1] *fath*] i.e. fetch.
[2] The moral is wanting in Hazl.

¶ Finis.

¶ Thus endeth the booke of a .C. mery talys. Empryntyd at London at the fygne of the Merymayd At Powlys gate next to chepe fyde. ¶ The yere of our Lorde .M. v. C. .xxvi. ¶ The .xxii. day of Nouēber.

JOHANNES RASTELL.

¶ Cum preuilegio
Regali.

www.ingramcontent.com/pod-product-compliance
Lightning Source LLC
Chambersburg PA
CBHW020251170426
43202CB00008B/322